KAṬHA-YOGA

Yadantah Tadupaasitavyam

(Which is inside, that is to be meditated upon)

Kaṭha-Yoga

Yadantah Tadupaasitavyam

(Which is inside, that is to be meditated upon)

DR. SIVANANDA MURTY

ADITYA PRAKASHAN
New Delhi

First published: 2009

ISBN 978-81-7742-091-3

Published by Aditya Prakashan, 2/18, Ansari Road, New Delhi – 110 002.
email: contact@adityaprakashan.com
website: www.adityaprakashan.com

Printed at Replika Press Pvt. Ltd.

Contents

Part II

Preface

It is six years since the first English version of my commentary was published. Dr. Frawley, the erudite scholar, author of many books on Astrology, and many Vedic subjects, has paid his attention to this. Another equally important contribution to this work is that of Mahamahopadhyaya, Prof. Sri Pullela Sriramachandrudu, who is one of the outstanding scholars we have in India today. A person with many excellent works on Vedanta, Darsanas and Sanskrit literature to his credit, he has enriched the Indian literature in an unprecedented manner and scale. It is my good fortune that he has made a critical study of my work both in its Telugu version and the English rendering presented here. He has given his learned opinion on this English version. I consider his opinion an authentication of this work of mine.

My valued friend and an eminent orientalist and author, Dr. Frawley has edited, rearranged and improved the clarity of the text with great care, making it readable to wider circles of readership. I cannot adequately thank him for his great contribution. The repetition of some ideas in the commentary could not be avoided due to demand of the context. I crave the reader's indulgence for such repetition. I consider it a great advantage that this work has received in the editing by Dr. Frawley.

After what I have received from Dr. Frawley and Dr. Sriramachandrudu, I have nothing more to ask for. It is the spiritual truth-content in this work that has to find a genuine readership and acceptance. The delay and any inadequacies are my own.

Dr. Sivananda Murty
Bheemunipatnam, Andhra Pradesh, India – 531 163
May 18 2008

Foreword

Dr. David Frawley (Pandit Vamadeva Shastri)

The *Upanishads* have formed the perennial fountainhead of Indian spirituality since well before the time of the Buddha. They have continued on throughout the centuries as the most enduring and dynamic portion of India's great Vedic heritage that goes back to the very dawn of human history. The *Upanishads* have inspired the innumerable great seers and yogis of the region and provided them with the basis for their numerous profound teachings and practices. The *Upanishads* present the prime Vedantic doctrines of *Atman* and *Brahman*, *Karma*, rebirth and liberation as well outlining as the prime Yogic methods of mantra and meditation that have long characterized this great spiritual tradition and which were adopted by later Buddhist and Jain teachings as well.

Yet there remains much ignorance about the *Upanishads* and their message and some mystery about their meaning. In the western world, the *Upanishads* are treated either as books of inspirational thoughts or as seeds of later rational philosophical systems, but they are rarely examined in their own right. They are regarded as the oldest texts of Indian philosophy, showing how it arose out of a Vedic ritualistic background, but there is little understanding of their Vedic basis and their deep connection with the mysterious Vedic *Mantras*.

The *Upanishads* are seldom looked upon as living teachings or of practical relevance for the spiritual life of people today in the modern world. Though Yoga is popular in the West, it is mainly the asana (postures) side that is followed and the *Upanishadic* basis of Yoga, though emphasized by many great Yogis from India, is seldom appreciated. Few Yoga teachers, much less students, have any real knowledge of these foundational texts of the very tradition that they may claim to be part of.

In India, the *Upanishads* are regarded as ancient scriptures and no doubt highly honored, but seldom studied in a serious manner as manuals of Yoga and meditation. They are usually looked upon as the source books for later philosophies of *Advaita* or *Dvaita*. Their commentaries have long assumed more importance than the actual texts, which few look directly into or care for in themselves. People are inclined to debate these rather long and abstruse commentaries, which often get caught up in secondary details, rather than to meditate upon the original texts and try to directly ascertain their meaning.

It can be argued that the *Upanishads* are the most important texts of all Indian teachings of all systems. They formed not only the foundation on which later Vedantic philosophy was built and the system of Yoga arose; they are also a mysterious door back into the Vedic world with its cryptic *Mantras* and luminous symbols that appeal more to an intuitive mind rather than to the logical intellect. In the *Upanishads*, both the Vedantic philosophy of the *Atman* and the Vedic symbology of fire and light coexist as one integral teaching that can communicate simultaneously to both the rational and intuitive aspects of our consciousness.

The Katha Upanishad

The *Katha* is perhaps the most interesting of the several shorter classical *Upanishads*. It is much easier to understand than older, longer and more Vedic *Upanishads* like the *Chandogya* and *Brihadaranyaka*, which reflect a more archaic Vedic language and symbolism. Yet the *Katha* has its own aura of mystery and still reflects many older Vedic ideas and practices.

Yama, the God of Death, is the main teacher or guru of this *Upanishad*, who instructs the youth *Nachiketa*. Death is often the great teacher in spiritual teachings throughout the world. Death is arguably our original teacher as it compels us to look more deeply into the meaning of our lives. On an inner level, God himself is the death of the ego. Many great deities like *Siva* and *Kali*, also represent death and transformation. Religion itself is mainly concerned with what, if anything in us, transcends death.

Death is the doorway to the world of the Gods or the immortals, the way beyond time and suffering. The God of Death or Yama in Vedic thought is also the twin brother of Manu, the primal man, representing death that is our constant companion and shadow throughout our brief mortal existence. Death or *Mrityu* is listed as one of the first great Upanishadic gurus in the *Brihadaranyaka* list of teachers. Indeed it can be said that the spiritual life itself is a kind of voluntary death and renunciation. The Vedic sacrifice is a ritualized death experience for those who perform it. Its main goal is to take us beyond death, which is also to take us through death to the other shore of eternity beyond it.

Yoga itself is a kind of inner death experience or practice. Death is symbolic of yogic methods of *Pranayama* and *Pratyahara* in which the yogi withdraws his prana from the physical body, and in a simulated death experience, dives deep into the Self within the heart. Ramana Maharshi, a modern Nachiketa like the youth of this *Upanishad*, records such a yogic death experience as the basis of his Self-realization that occurred when he was a mere lad of sixteen. To find the deathless Self, we must first pass through death. We must die while living in order to discover the life beyond death.

Nachiketa represents the pure mind which seeks only to know the truth and cannot be distracted by the many other desires and pursuits that characterize the ordinary human world. This pure mind voluntarily goes to the house of death.

It sees the inherent impermanence of life and is not taken in by life's alluring appearances. It voluntarily seeks death, knowing that to be the only real way beyond this world and its sorrow.

When one goes voluntarily to the house of death, like Nachiketa, one will find that there is no one home. Death only exists for those who are unwilling to die, who cannot give up their attachment to the body and the external world, which makes death real and final for them. Furthermore, when one goes voluntarily to the house of death, he becomes a guest, no longer under the power of death. Death no more has any claim over him. He becomes someone that death does not control but even death must honor. For him, the God of death becomes the great guru or teacher.

The three days that Nachiketa stayed in the house of death were without the owner of that house noticing him. It shows that the one who dies voluntarily cannot immediately be seen by death. He can experience death without having to be consumed by it. In that period, death changes his nature for him. While for ordinary men, death collects his debts and karmas, for spiritually awakened seekers like Nachiketa, who can face and endure death, death becomes a giver of gifts. What causes this change? When we give up our pursuit of karma or results and pursue knowledge instead, then our debts and karmas disappear or turn into knowledge. When the true seeker voluntarily dies, then death becomes a giver of the highest knowledge and the greatest boons. Perhaps no other story in the spiritual literature of the world so reveals this truth as this short *Upanishad*.

Nachiketa himself is a manifestation of *Agni*, the fire child, *Kumara*, our own inner child of immortality, which is why a special sacred fire or *Nachiketa Agni* is consecrated to him. He is also *Sanat Kumara* or the eternal child who never dies — the Divine soul and seeking of absolute truth within us. He is *Skanda*, the causal guru mentioned in the *Chandogya Upanishad*. Fire is the deity through whom we die, not simply as the power that cremates the body but also as power that purifies the mind and heart, the burning up of the ego and its *Samskaras* in the fire of knowledge (*Jnanagni*).

The *Upanishad* provides the teachings of yogic dying that take us beyond *karma* and rebirth. As it is short and to the point, it has retained its prestige over longer and more circuitous teachings. It remains a practical manual for going beyond time and desire.

Sivananda Murty

India has a long tradition of great teachers who used the *Upanishads* to express their insights and to awaken their disciples. Sivananda Murty is one of the most important of such modern masters. Though widely known in Andhra Pradesh, the region of India where he lives, he is little known in the West, which is generally still not able to discriminate between genuine spiritual yogis and mere *yogaasana* technicians.

Sivananda Murty is unique in that he has the knowledge of Yoga and its inner practices, as well as the knowledge of *Advaita* and *Jnana*. In addition, he understands both the Vedic and Puranic traditions along with their main mantra and meditation practices. While there are many people East and West today who can talk about *Advaita*, which often gets reduced to a kind of 'instant enlightenment' fad, there are very few who actually know the way to achieve that supreme state by really going beyond death and transcending body consciousness. Few know the yogic methods that are usually essential for this transformation. In this regard, Sivananda Murty provides an example and a way to follow that restores the depth to these ancient teachings meant to really take us to the eternal, not merely as a belief or conviction but as a realization of our entire being.

Murtyji has chosen what is perhaps the most classical spiritual story of India, that of the Katha Upanishad, but has looked at it in a much deeper light than even the great

Advaitic commentators of the past. He has elucidated it with the insights of *Jnana*, Yoga and Karma (ritual) combined, revealing all the layers of its manifold secrets back to its Vedic roots. He hasn't reduced the text to one level only. He hasn't simply used the text to reflect his own ideas or to promote a philosophical system but to stimulate the genuine seeker to real Yoga practices and introspection of the deepest kind. This makes his interpretation unique and of special interest to all those who value the *Upanishads.* It brings the *Upanishads* back to life as living teachings, transporting one almost back in time into the Upanishadic age.

Perhaps most importantly Murtyji shows how Vedic rituals can be important to the path of *Jnana* or Self-realization, either as external practices or as internal rituals and Yoga practices. He does this not by reducing knowledge to ritual, but showing the secret knowledge that can work through ritual and elevate it to a meditative act. In this way he restores an older Vedic approach that used ritual as a means of taking us to knowledge, neither denying its efficacy, nor reducing the pursuit of knowledge to it. He also shows how ritual can be used as an aid to win the higher worlds, even in absence of the seeking for complete liberation.

I have had the good fortune and grace to meet with Sivananda Murty on several occasions over the past ten years and to experience several aspects of his teaching and insight that cover almost every domain of Vedic and yogic thought and practice. This current Upanishadic book represents only one side of his vast knowledge. It has been my honor to go over this book and make adjustments of language when necessary to improve its communication. Hopefully, I have not anywhere interfered with its meaning or added anything extraneous.

The Purusha in the Heart

The Vedic ritual or *Yajna* is centred on Agni or the sacred fire, starting with the first verse of the *Rigveda* itself of *Agnim Ile.*

Yet this Vedic ritual is not simply external (bahiryajna) on a fire altar but also internal (antaryajna), in our own minds, or on the altar of our own hearts. So too, the Vedic fire is both outward (adhibhoutic) and inward (adhyatmic), both a material and a spiritual reality.

The outer ritual worships the Divine with external substances like ghee and rice, which are placed into a fire started through wood and other flammable material substances. The inner ritual worships the Self in the heart by making internal offerings of body, speech and mind to the indwelling Divine fire, the flame of our own being and consciousness. The ultimate offering of this internal Self-sacrifice or *Atma-Yajna* is to offer one's own mind and ego to the Divine, to consciously die into immortality. It is this inner sacrifice that we see in the story of the Katha Upanishad.

The Purusha in the heart is Agni, who is our inner child or Kumara. This Kumara in its human form is Nachiketa. This inner fire is not fire as a mere element but the Purusha as the indwelling light of consciousness, a light that is circumscribed by the body into a flame the size of a thumb, the *Angusthamatra Purusha*, or the person the size of a thumb of the *Upanishads*. This thumb size light is also the linga, the pillar of light that is the subtle body or *sukshma Sarira*. The essential teaching of the Katha Upanishad is this mergence into the Self that manifests through the heart.

The Mahanarayana *Upanishad* makes this relationship clear in its famous Narayana *Sukta*. It speaks of the lotus of the heart as containing a great fire (Mahan Agni) that is responsible for bodily heat and supports the digestive fire in the stomach. In this flame is a streak of lightning at its crest which is the *Jivatman* or reincarnating soul, whose continual spark lights this fire and keeps it going. At the top of this lightning is the bindu, point or dot of the *Paramatman*, the supreme Self that is never born and never dies. Unfortunately, most commentators take this as a mere visual description for meditation and miss its profound reality as describing the soul in the heart.

Our spiritual journey is to return to this fire in the heart, to the lightning hidden behind it that is our real soul and finally to the point of pure light behind that, which is our true Self and Supreme Being. That point is the doorway to the infinite, the way beyond all darkness and sorrow. Only if we first become very small can we become vast. This requires that we die to the body, the mind and the external world. Death is that point of purification we must pass through in order to gain entrance into the world of eternity and infinity. Yoga teaches us various methods to accomplish this process that is the real journey of our souls from darkness to light.

Sivananda Murty in explaining the Katha Upanishad makes this process clear and relevant for all of us. We are grateful to him for clearing away the dust of time and the confusion of philosophers, and once more connecting us with the essential Upanishadic wisdom that is the soul of India and perhaps our most ancient and eternal way of Self-knowledge as a species. His book provides new light on the *Upanishads* and shows us how to use Yoga and Vedanta together to practically achieve our highest goals.

Dr. David Frawley (Pandit Vamadeva Shastri)
Santa Fe, New Mexico, USA
March 2003

KATHA-YOGA: An Appreciation

Pullela Sriramachandrudu

"There is no philosophic system, except that of the Carvakas, which does not give greatest importance to yoga as a means of achieving the highest goal of human life" declares Sri Vidyaranya in the *Jivanmuktiviveka.* The importance of yoga as the highest spiritual discipline can be known from the fact that, while there are a few *Upanishads* exclusively dealing with yoga and are therefore called '*yogopanishads*', there are direct or indirect references to this system in all the other *Upanishads* also suggesting that every aspirant for *Moksha* has to invariably go through this discipline.

Kathopanishad occupies an important place in the Upanishadic literature. Though small in size with 120 *mantras*, it teaches the nature of the *Atman* with the indication of important means for its realisation by introducing a small but highly interesting story which runs as follows:

One great sage, Auddalaka performed a sacrifice and at the end he was giving away cows to the priests as *Dakshina*, the grateful honorarium. On seeing that some of the cows were emaciated by old age and were good for nothing, his son, Nachiketas, a lad in his teen age, went to his father and asked him — "Father! To whom are you going to give me?" When he did not get reply from his father, he repeated the same question twice or thrice. The father was annoyed and said, "I shall give you to the god of death". The son was perhaps expecting his father to ask him why he was putting such question, when he could reveal his mind to him. It did not happen. The father was in a different mood and he said something unexpected. Now the son insisted that he should go to the god of death in order to save his father from being a liar. He reached the abode of Yama, the god of death. It is not clear from the *Upanishad* whether he went or was sent. Yama was away from his city for three days. On returning to his place, Yama found Nachiketas waiting for him all those three days without food and proper reception. He apologised to him and offered him three *varas* (boons) to compensate his neglect for three days.

As the first *vara* (boon), Nachiketas requested Yama to see that his father would pardon him for his impertinence and recognise and receive him with affection when he goes back to his place. The *vara* (boon) was granted. Nachiketas must have heard that Yama was proficient in the *Agnividya* by the power of which he might have been holding such a highly powerful office in the heaven. He, therefore, requested him to teach the *Agnividya* as the second *vara*. While readily granting it, Yama, as an additional favour, said that the *Agnividya* would be known, thereafter, after Nachiketas' name. Nachiketas, then, requested for the third *vara* (boon) the granting of which requires the teaching of the nature of *Atman*. "After the death of a man something survives, some people say; nothing remains, say others; I beseech you, O! Revered god! To explain the correct position" — he posed a problem which can be tackled only by Yama. Granting this *vara* also Yama explained the nature of *Jivatman* and *Paramatman*. As an important means of realizing the Supreme Being, he taught many intricacies of yoga also. This, in brief, is the story of Nachiketas, which reflects the main contents of the *Upanishad*.

Here a few important questions arise:

(1) How did Nachiketas go to Yamaloka, the abode of god of death, and how could he expect to go back to his place after once he kicked the mortal Coil ?

(2) What is the purpose and relevance of Agnividya in an Upanishad, which is expected to teach only about the Atman?

(3) What is the type of yoga that was taught by Yama, which is considered to be the direct means of realising Atman ?

These are the questions, answers to which can be found only by a discerning mind purified by yogic practices and by *constant manana,* contemplation, as that of Satguru Sivananda Murtyji.

It is not irrelevant to narrate an important incident connected with Satguruji when he was in his teen age, perhaps the age of Nachiketas when he met his celestial Guru. This incident tells us how a great Yogin concealed in him was brought out by a great holy personality of spiritual eminence. When Satguruji was taking his morning bath in the holy river Godavari near the historical bridge which was of about three miles length at Kovvur, at the western bank of the river, a revered Yogin appeared before him and bade him to receive a mantra, the *siddhi* (fruition) of which could be realised by one day's *tapas* (mental repetition). Thus he appeared on 32 consecutitive days and gave 32 *Mantras* and the *siddhi* of which mantra was obtained by Satguruji on the same day of receiving it from the revered Yogin. It was like Viswamitra transferring powerful *Astras* to the young Rama. One of those days, Satguruji asked him "why are you doing all this?". "You are not an ordinary lad", said the Yogin; "you are a great Yogin destined to help the revival of Sanatana Dharma and kindle the light of spirituality in thousands of yearning hearts. Shortly you are going to have the vision of the thousand-hooded Adisesha. You should not show any sign of fear on seeing him; lest you should lose your life." Everything happened as was predicted; one day Satguruji had the vision of the Lord of Serpents who was as long as the bridge on the river Godavari. In a few moments, He disappeared into the person of Satguruji.

Satguruji hails from the Zamindary family of Urlam of the northern region of Andhra Pradesh which has been engaged for many generations in the Shatkalapuja (worshipping six times everyday) of the Lord Parama Siva, the Adiyogin and the yoga preceptor of the world, and patronising the Vedas and Sastras by conducting annual conferences of the Vedic scholars and honouring the deserving, a practice, which was prevalent throughout India in the families of Rajas and Zamindars before the advent of independence; and which was not found in any other country in the world. No wonder, a great Yogin of Satguruji's eminence and stature has appeared in such a pious family.

The prophecy of the Yogin who met Satguruji on the banks of Godavari has become true. Ever since Satguruji has been leading pious life of a Yogin, without donning saffron clothes but being engaged in *loka-sangraha* (welfare of the world), guiding the seekers in spiritual paths, like the sages and *Jnanis* of yore (like Vasistha, Viswamitra and Janaka) who never left the worldly activities and continued to stay in *grihasthashrama*, the stage of life of a householder. As part of many efforts for preserving the main tenets of the *Sanathanadharma*, he gives lectures on topics connected with Indian Culture and on the problems being faced by this ancient *Dharma* in the contemporary world, encourages arts like music and dance connected with the Indian Culture by holding periodical conferences and concerts in which persons, proficient in these arts participate and also adequately honoured, conducts every year grand functions in which persons of eminence in different fields like literature, science and administration are honoured, arranges performances of *Yaagas* in all the Kshetras (Holy places) situated through out this great country seeking the grace of the Lord Siva for the welfare of the world (*Viswasanti*) and writes and publishes articles and books on ancient Indian literature and *Sanathanadharma*. Satguruji is one of the great Yogins who look at the world as one family with no distinction of caste, creed, race, region or country.

Katha-Yoga is one of such important works from the pen of Satguruji. Satguruji delivered series of lectures, about 30 years ago, to his devotees which were collected in a consolidated form into a book and were published in Telugu a few years ago which are now being published in English. In this work, the contents of Kathopanishad are critically analysed with the explanation of their significance. In this work, we get answers to the above questions and many more points connected with Brahmavidya and yogic practices.

The sage Auddalaka gave away all his possessions to the priests and other Vedic scholars. Though in his fit of annoyance he said that he would give away his son to the god of death, who was neither a priest nor a Vedic scholar, he had no right to do so, because the children and wives cannot be considered as mere property to be given away to others at one's will. (Katha-Yoga 3.2 (K.Y. 3.2)). Nachiketas knew it. But to save his father's honour, he wanted to present himself before Yama; he went to Yama's abode. But he was never dead; in which case Yama would have had prior information about his arrival; and he would not have also been obliged to receive him as the most honoured guest. How did, then, Nachiketas go to *Yamaloka*? As explained by Satguruji. Nachiketas went to *Yamaloka* with his *Sukshmasarira* (subtle body) leaving his *Sthulasarira* (gross material body) at a safe place so that he could enter it after he returned, about which he did not have any doubt. A portion of pranic power was left behind so that the *Sthulasarira* (gross body) did not get decomposed. A Yogi can enter into another body, dead or alive, leaving his own body behind for some period. This is a very rare feat known only to the Indian Yogins and it is called *Parakayapravesa*. This has been explained by Satguruji with all the details of the procedure in the yogic language (K.Y. 7.2). in the present case, of course, there is no *Parakayapravesa*. Nachiketas appeared before Yama with his *Sukshmasarira*. "This *Upanishad* proves that such a state is possible in which a soul can continue as an individual beyond the body or go out of its body without dying – leaving the body temporarily behind with life, but no soul. It also proves that an individual soul can travel as he wishes, out side the body, if there is a premeditated *Sankalpa* and yogic power to do this." (K.Y. 3.1)

Yama's absence when Nachiketas visited his place, has become a cause of anxiety for Him (Yama), but this unexpected leisure of three days was wisely used by Nachiketas for a better purpose. Yama was worried that he might lose all his power and wealth because it was said –"If at anybody's household a brahmin guest waits in expectation for food but is not cared for, all the merits of that foolish householder, whether from speaking truth, sacrificial offerings, association with great men, or wealth of cattle and progeny will go to that guest himself" (K.Y. Text 1.1.8). What was offered by Nachiketas to Yama, at the end as *Gurudakshina* for having received instructions in the spiritual path, we do not know. Of course no spiritual guru would expect anything from his *sisya* (offering to the preceptor) disciple, excepting his steady progress in the spiritual path. But the Guru here, had to offer *sisyadakshina*, as it were, to Nachiketas, says Satguruji, "Strangely, the guru, here seems to have become indebted to the disciple, paying his debt as it were, for an omission in hospitality to the disciple". (K.Y. 1.6)

But Nachiketas was the gainer here. He used those three days as an opportunity for performing penance, on account of which only he could, when an offer came from Yama, think of those *varas*, the last two of which were very important not only for himself but for the whole humanity. This is indicated by Satguruji when he writes — "Three nights of waiting, obviously, was the *Tapas* required before having a vision of the God-Guru. After all, *Tapas* has to be ultimately defined as keen waiting for the ultimate experience with *Sadhana* or devotion for the object sought, faith in the achievement and total trust in the Guru's grace". (K.Y. 3.1). "Guru also has no other option excepting to give instruction in spiritual path to a highly deserving disciple", says Satguruji, indicating how strong the spiritual knot between the *Sisya* and Guru is. "The threatened loss of wealth of the God-Guru indicates how the god or guru has no freedom not to give what is sought by an eminently eligible disciple." (K.Y. 3.1). These words remind one of the statements of Sri Sankaracharya who said in his *Bhashya* on Prasnopanishad — "No teacher proficient in the subject should deny instruction to a sincere student and utter a lie that he does not know the subject".

Ato Nyaayata Upasannaaya yogyaaya jaanataa vidyaa vaktavyaiva

anrtaram ca na vaktvyam sarvaasvavyavasthaasu ityetat siddham bhavaati" (P.U. 6.1)

Vedic rituals (*Yaagas*) are said to be *Araadupa kaarakah*, useful from a distance, i.e., indirectly, in producing *Atmajnaana*, the knowledge of one's own self as identical with the Supreme Being.

"Tametam vedaanuaccanena braahmana vividisanti yajnena, daanena, tapasaanaasakena" (Br. U. 4.4.22).

There are two types of *Yaaga–Bahiryaaga* and *Antaryaaga*. The *Yaaga*, which is actually performed using all the required things on specified number of days and times, is *Bahiryaaga*, external sacrifice. The Yaaga performed through mental process, imagining different objects as the different things prescribed for *Yaaga* is *Antaryaaga*, internal sacrifice; it comes under Yoga and is more powerful as a means of Atmajnaana, than the *Bahiryaaga*. This is an important point explained by Satguruji on the authority of many texts on this subject. While explaining the greatness of *Asvamedha* (horse sacrifice) as an *Antaryaaga*, he writes: "...humans who offer a horse to Prajapati satisfy all the gods. Those who perform such a sacrifice understandingly and meaningfully conquer death forever. For this they must realise that the real horse that is offered is their own qualified self and its attendants... The *Jivatman* can also attain the Supreme *Brahman* through it by further meditation without ritual". (K.Y. 4.4).

What is said of the *Antaryaaga* of Aswamedha is true in the case of the *Viswajityaaga* and the *Nachiketayaaga*. The later is more powerful when it is combined with the meditation on 'Omkaara' — "This prescription of the *Nachiketayajna* by Yama, named after the boy, could grant long and fruitful life on earth, a higher world as desired by the performer and ultimate salvation through meditation on Pranava, (OM)". (K.Y. 2.2.). "This ritual of the *Nachiketavidya* is not very elaborate when compared to others like the Viswajit; but it additionally demands knowledge of Yoga along with a strong desire for Liberation." (K.Y. 2.2).

As a third boon, Yama explains the nature of *Atman*, both in its delimited form as Jiva and in its real form as an all pervading *Paramatman* or *Brahman*. There are three passages in the Kathopanishad which describe *Atman* as being of the size of *Angushta*, the thumb, being situated in the cavity of the heart of a human being. (K.U 2.1.12; 2.1.13; and 2.1.17). This is both *Jivatman* and *Paramatman*. As a being delimited by the cavity of the heart, the seat of the *Antahkarana*, internal organ, it is Jiva and taken as an all pervading being after separating it from the *Antahkarana*, it is *Paramatman*. Every Saadhana is meant for the realisation of the identity of these so called two beings. This point is explained by Satguruji in the following words — "What makes *Atman* an individual in the body is none else than the existence of an entity called the Angushtapurusha, which means a person who is of the size of the thumb. Because of his miniature size we can call him the 'inch-man'... This *Jivatman* in its true primordial state is none other than the *Paramatman* Himself." ... "Isvara or God must also be present within the human body. Consciousness (Citta) is working as *Jivatman*. Thus, the *Paramatman* is surrounded by the ethereal body-reflection and endowed with limited consciousness in the man. This *Paramatman* is a 'dimensionless dot' of light within the Jiva, in its heart-centre. His effulgent presence enables the *Jivatman* to function in the body. For this reason, the Angushtapurusha is very often described as the *Paramatman* himself." ... "The inner *Paramatman* is the true reality and *Jivatman* is but a relative, fleeting, impermanent and dependent reality. Therefore, that One *Paramatman* reflects Himself in all living bodies in their respective shapes accompanied by their respective egos and their accompanying body-consciousness. He is an enduring all time Truth meaning that he is deathless and changeless." (K.Y. 4.2). A beautiful summary of the main teachings of the *Upanishad*!

Yama taught the path of ritual-yoga combination and also pure yogic *Sadhana* for experiencing the highest truth, the identity of *Jivatman* and *Paramatman*." The Kathopanishad offers such a unique path of ritual yoga combination in which the ritual helps conquer the evil results of physical death granting an uninterrupted continuity of the self-same consciousness of the Yogi. The *Upanishad* also offers yoga as a superior and exclusive path to *Moksha* by adherence to the Pranava, OM, in the yogic heart-centre. With yoga as the inner sacrifice to complement the outer or ritual sacrifice, a complete path is offered." (K.Y. 4.4).

Even without the help of the rituals one can overcome death and attain *Moksha* by the *Upasana* done through the concentration of mind on *Anghata chakra*. "In the message of the Katha *Upanishad*, the Lord of Death is pointing to the secret of the *Anaahata*, accompanied by the Pranava, OM, as the gateway to final dissolution" (K.Y. 5.5). As a great Yogin with practical experience, Satguruji explains the procedure of the *Upasana* of *Anaahata*: "The *Yogasaastra* describes this *Anaahata* as a twelve petalled lotus... he (Yogin) should imagine such a lotus with twelve petals in the heart-centre and circumambulate it with his mind, dwelling one by one on the sounds of its different letters from 'Kam' to 'Tham'. This dwelling on sound of the petals in repeated conscious circumambulations must be done adequately to obtain oneness with the sounds. Dwelling on such sounds means with full attention inwardly, not that one should physically utter them. It means that one should try to hear them within in a state of silence. This is done, of course, with controlled breath. Such is the mental utterance." (K.Y. 5.5)

This *Upanishad* is named after the *Anaahata chakra*, marked with 12 mantraas (letters) 'ka' to 'ttha', maintains Satguruji. "Since the very subject matter of the *Upanishad* is *Anaahata* we can even infer that the *Upanishad* is named as 'Katha' after the *Mantras* of the heart-centre" (K.Y. 5.5). This explains the significance of the name of the present work 'Katha-Yoga'. The Vedic text itself derives its name on account of this Kathopanishad. "It is significant to note that this 'V*edasakha*' had the name of '*Kathasakha*' because of its containing Katha *Upanishad* therein." (K.Y. Intro. P.1). Satguruji is aware of "the tradition that traces the name of a *Rsi* after whom Katha is given as the name of the relevant portion of the Veda." (K.Y. 7.5).

Vedic *Mantras* and words are capable of being interpreted in different ways as can be seen from different authors, at times by the same author himself. Thus we find the well-known Mantra – '*chatvaari sringa*', '*trayosya pada*' etc. (R.V. 4.58.3) having been interpreted differently by different commentators. It is interpreted by Nirukta as a mantra praising the god Agni as Yajnapurusha. This mantra is found in a *Sukta*, which has five Devataas — *agni*, *surya*, *aapah* (water), *go (*earth*)* and *ghrita* (ghee or butter oil). While commenting on this, Sri Sayanacharya says — "on account of its situation in a particular *Rik*, it is to be interpreted in five different ways as applicable to the five Devaas." After these remarks, he interpreted it as referring to two gods, Agni as Yajnapurusha and the Sun. This same mantra is interpreted by Patanjali in the *Mahabhashya* as extolling the greatness of *Vyakarana*. This same *Rik* is interpreted by Rajasekhara of 9th century, in his *Kavyamimamsa*, as referring to the *Saahityasaastra*.

There is a tradition of naming certain parts of Veda after the subject discussed in that part. Thus that part of the Veda where the *Agnicayana*, (a sacrifice where the bricks are to be arranged in a particular manner) is discussed is called 'Agni'. There is a phrase "*Saagni adhite*" which means he studies the Veda up to the end of the Agni grantha. "*Agnigranthaparyantham adhite saagni*" explains Siddhanta Kaumudi. Baalamanoramaa, the commentary, says: "here 'Agni' means that part of the work in which Agni is discussed (Siddhantha Kaumudi with Baalamanoramaa, Avyayibhaava prakarana under Sutra "Avyayam vibhuthi" etc. 2.1.6). In view of all this, the new interpretation of the word 'katha' is very appropriate as it suggests the importance of *Anaahatavidya*, contained in this *Upanishad*. It also shows a kind of *samanvaya* (conciliation) between the *Upanishad* and Aagamic traditions.

In the course of examining the main contents of the *Upanishad*, Satguruji has dealt with many topics of yogic importance such as *Praanaayaama*, three *Granthis* (knots), some of the rare yogic experiences, the state of deathlessness, the six *chakraas*, *Kundalini*, five *Kosaas*, the procedure involved in leaving one body and entering another, the *Sukshmasarira*, the three *naadis*—*ida*, *pingala*, and *sushumna*, and their functions and several other things which require careful study even for a theoretical understanding. The additional comments (commentaries) on the *Mantras* of the first two *vallis* (cantos) and those selected from the other portions of the *Upanishad* throw much light on several aspects of yoga and on the nature of *Atman* and bodies. The 6th and 7th sections of about 40 pages form the essence of this great treatise. This work is sure to kindle interest in the minds of the *Astikas* (believers) on a great subject which has been unfortunately neglected by the generations of Indians, who without realising what a great treasure they are missing, are running after the mirage of worldly comforts. There are, of course, many scholars but most of them are engaged in dry debates neglecting the practical aspects of our great philosophical systems and the Yoga. Satguruji has a word for them, "... since Sri Sankara expounded his profound *Advaita* philosophy... there has been a spate of argumentative expositions by scholars for or against the theory of *Advaita*. All such literature is certainly a treat for the well-educated intellectual... But to the common man in Hindu society, today, who is seeking guidance for spiritual practice, these abstruse philosophies, monism or dualism are like Greek and Latin". "Commonplace and simple Hindu methods of worship, a devotional path in life and a revival of temple culture in society are what is required to satisfy the needs of most people today" (K.Y. 2.6). As was already mentioned, it is to achieve this end that Satguruji has been engaged, day and night, for the last 50 years.

All paths of spirituality are complimentary to each other, not different paths leading to different places, declares Satguruji in another place. "We should realise that Vedic ritualism, yogic knowledge of the secrets of the physical Creation, the Cosmological secrets revealed in Saankhya, the Vedantic explanation of *Brahman*, and the theories about God contained in the *Upanishads* are all complimentary to each other and not different paths. They should be understood together as one total subject. This must be obvious to us because all these teachings are derived from Veda in its four sectional contents of *Samhita*, *Brahmana*, *Aranyaka* and *Upanishad*. It would be wrong to the pure philosopher dwelling on the secrets of the unqualified *Brahman* as a means of *Moksha* to dismiss the *Yoga-Sankhya* combination or the Yoga-ritual combination as incorrect or unhelpful." (K.Y. 4.4).

While revealing some of the secrets of Yoga and *Jnaana* contained in the Kathopanishad, in this very important work Katha-Yoga of unique nature, it is important and unique because many personal experiences of a Yogin are enshrined in this. Satguruji exhorts us to lead a pious and simple life without creating schisms in this great Hindu society in the name of conflicting philosophical speculations, creeds, God or gods. (K.Y. 2.6).

I consider it as an act of great Anugraha on the part of Satguru Sri Sivananda Murty ji in giving an opportunity to write a few lines on this great work, to fathom the depths of which is beyond the capacity of persons like me of theoretical smattering of the subject such as Yoga and Jnaana. I offer my sincere Pranaams to him who is a living example for what is said in the following sloka of *Bhagavadgita* (with one word changed):

"Namesti kinchit kartavyam trisu lokesu kinchana,
Naanavaaptamavaaptavyam varta eva ca karmani".

P. Sriramachandrudu
Hyderabad
July 31 2005

Introduction

This commentary on Katha Upanishad is an attempt to prepare the reader to understand and appreciate the subtleties and secret messages contained in this Upanishad. Unlike other Upanishads, this Upanishad contains an episode, a happening, the performance of a Yajna, the accompanying charity and a little boy questioning his father to know to whom he himself would be gifted away along with the resultant annoyance of the father and an unmeant curse. All these ingredients present an unplanned incident described as the background of the Upanishad. Nachiketa's meeting with Yama, the God of Death, his brief interview with him, and what has transpired from it require a deeper analysis.

The incident itself is far from natural. Hence, it has to be explained what exactly was meant by Nachiketa traveling, waiting and meeting with Yama and finally returning to his father. This has been explained in the chapter "*Yoga – Chakras and Kundalini* (Chapter 7)". Yama's boon is a kind of initiation that leads to unraveling the mystery of creation which is the very secret sought by Nachiketa. The *mantra* part of the initiation is only *Omkara* which is neither new nor unprecedented. But then the tacit path indicated is the *Anahata chakra*. Here lies the great secret meaning of the very name or title of the Upanishad, KATHA. *Anahata chakra* contains a twelve petalled Lotus which are the seats of twelve mystic syllables, "*Ka*" to "*Ttha*". This is the hidden secret of Yama's path, which is secretly embedded in the very title of the Upanishad. This commentary is chiefly meant to unravel this mystery.

This work is in two parts. The first part consisting of chapters 1 through 7 is aimed at providing the reader with the necessary foundation to go through the text proper.

Chapter I: The mysterious phenomenon of Death, the death-experience and the possibility of escaping the pain of death and death itself, thereby achieving a continuity of the inner-man are explained in this chapter.

Chapter II: The Vedic tradition consisting of an external ritual with its spiritual meaning are explained. The 'Oneness' and the complimentary nature of the Vedic ritual and Vedanta are brought out in this chapter.

Chapter III: The strange incident of Nachiketa traveling to the 'world of souls' is explained to prove the reality of the various Vedantic and Upanishadic assertions.

Chapter IV: This chapter deals with the subtle body which is the in-dweller, who uses the instrument of the physical body in this earthly life. The famous historic *Aswamedha* as a technological means of the performer merging him with the Prajapati is also explained in this.

Chapter V: The *Nachiketagni*, a new invention, taught by Yama which is the combination of the rite and the spirit is explained in this chapter.

Chapter VI: The already existing paths to emancipation like the Samkhya and the Brahma Sutras and the path of Devotion are explained here.

Chapter VII: We hear stories of *Parakaya pravesha vidya*, namely the *yogi* entering into another human body and acting therein. The secret science involved in this is briefly placed before the reader. This chapter contains the very heart of this Upanishad, namely the *Anahata Chakra*. The name of the Upanishad is for the first time derived from the mystic syllables contained in the Lotus of the Yogic Centre, *Anahata*; "*Ka*" as the first and the "*Ttha*", the last of the twelve syllables on the Lotus.

In the second part, the first three of the six sections (*Vallis*) of the Upanishad are commented upon in detail. The other three *Vallis* are summarized briefly.

Mere philosophical explanation for the sake of establishing an *advaitic* view may not justify the birth of this unique Upanishad. This Upanishad would then become redundant in the presence of other purely philosophical Upanishads. Hence Kathopanishad is unquestionably establishing a yogic path for the conquering of death and to the final absorption in Brahman. Here is an effort to establish Yoga as a path leading to a direct experience of the ultimate truth, often described as '*aparokshanubhuti*' rather than a '*parokshanubhuti*' or an indirect semblance of experience by an intellectual understanding of the ultimate truth or otherwise.

It is thus, the Upanishad more appropriately deserves to be called Katha-Yoga.

1. The Phenomenon of Death

The Katha Upanishad is one of the most important of the shorter *Upanishads* and is perhaps the most known and most quoted among these revered ancient texts. No one can claim to understand the *Upanishad* without having studied it closely. Indeed all the secrets of Yoga and Vedanta can be found within its handful of profound verses. It has a great and unique power that can attract and guide seekers even today.

The Katha Upanishad originally formed an appendix to the *Brahmana* of the *Katha Sakha* of the *Krishna Yajurveda*. Some trace it to the *Sama Veda* or the *Atharva Veda* as well. However, the portions of the *Vedas* containing this *Upanishad* have been lost in the long course of time, like so many other texts. This *Upanishad*, as presenting the story of Nachiketa, is also called the *Nachiketa Upanishad.* The story of Nachiketa is found with some variations in the *Mahabharata.* So it is a common and famous Vedic tale, with deep meaning and profound implications.

The *Krishna Yajurveda* had four *Sakhas* (branches), one of which is the *Katha Sakha.* The *Brahmana* of this *Sakha* is not completely available. But it is significant to note that this *Sakha* had the name *Kathaka Sakha* because of its containing Katha Upanishad therein.

Just as in the other portions of the *Krishna Yajurveda*, a clear demarcation between *Brahmana* and *Aranyaka* (the ritual and meditation portions) is not found in this *Sakha* either. Some scholars say that the word '*Krishna*' — indicating darkness or vagueness of the *Brahmana* and *Aranyaka* demarcation — is responsible for the name *Krishna-Yajurveda*.

1.1 Escape from Death

Every living being is certain only about one thing, its eventual death. Yet in spite of the fact that death is a common phenomenon occurring everywhere in the world, the process of death remains a deep mystery. This is owing to the thick curtain that separates our present life from the after-life. The belief in an after-life, but with a complete ignorance as to what it really is, is responsible for the fear of death that is perhaps our greatest fear. It is the fear of the unknown. Those who shun this fear prefer to disbelieve and try to reject any idea of an after-life with their self-imposed logic, claiming that beyond this world there is nothing. But this fear is inescapably inherent in us. Indifference to the question or mere prayer to the God, one believes in, are the main alternatives to really dealing with it.

However, in the past another class of men (including Asuric personalities like Ravana) resorted to penance seeking absolute deathlessness for their physical bodies. While they could not get a complete reprieve against physical death, they could achieve the most improbable conditions for it, which guaranteed them near immortality. And yet when these conditions were all eventually satisfied they had to meet with death anyway. They lived their lives in the self-assurance that they could really avoid death but only succeeded in delaying it. They only proved the futility of a merely long life.

Purely philosophical literature on this subject does not afford any insight or even a mild experience of this mysterious truth. One purpose of the *Katha Upanishad* is to explain death and after-life tacitly, to dispel the wrong notions about death, and allay the fears caused by ignorance about it. However, the ultimate purpose sought to be achieved in this *Upanishad* is conquering death, not merely by continuing to live in a physical body but by continuing to live beyond the body, acquiring mastery over oneself and living in a higher world or worlds of knowledge without the fear of dying again and obtaining salvation from the cycle of rebirths. A path of liberation (*Moksha*) to be practically followed by the soul beyond its body after conquering death is definitely indicated in the *Upanishad*.

1.2 The Experience of Death

No doubt, men follow many paths desiring salvation (as they conceive it to be). Yet every path a person may follow ends abruptly with his death. As rebirth is a result of Karma, the new surroundings and conditions of his next incarnation are beyond his control. One is bound to forget the past desires, goals and even the spiritual practices engaged in during ones previous life. The dawning of a desire once again for *Moksha* is only one of many possible events that can happen in the next life. It can only occur when the good and positive *Samskaras* (tendencies) of the previous birth weakly linger in the inner recesses of consciousness amidst the din and confusion of the new material living. But if such a *Samskara* is mild, it may survive birth after birth only as a weaker voice in consciousness, but never reach its fulfillment, in the absence of its exclusive presence.

An intense desire for *Moksha* is itself a result of traversing this very slow and circuitous path, life after life in nature, every time fraught with diversions and pitfalls. It is, therefore, necessary that once there is a real desire for release, care should be taken so that it is not thwarted by inevitable death only to be forgotten, waiting again for its chance revival. Death, therefore, is the most undesirable obstacle in the continuity of the path of liberation.

1.3 The Soul's Permanence and the Individual's Impermanence

Whose continuity is it anyway? The individual who desires liberation should necessarily continue to exist. The soul is not always the same body-owning, body-conscious, ego-centered individual. The soul is a different individual in that sense, every time it is reborn. Death is an enemy to the continuous survival of the true individual and his desires and therefore should be conquered. Hence, the question arises, 'What is meant by conquering death?'

Human beings are known as mortals. Ordinarily corporeal death is unconquerable. Death is the consequence of man's identifying himself with his perishable body in the deep belief and trust that he is alive only while he is in it. This results in belief in death. Death is an inevitable event whose distance is limited and proximity unlimited. It is coming to us eventually but may come to us anywhere and at any time. The experience of death is not even intellectually known to men since one who has died cannot come back to describe his experience to others. There are many things that must be experienced in order to be understood, like the vision of God. Death is such an experience the description of which is not available to us.There are cases of Yogis who experience a semblance of death by what is commonly described as an 'out of body experience' (O.B.E). Recently *Bhagavan Ramana Maharshi* experienced it. *Shirdi Sai Baba* also left his body for three days and then returned. But these are only exceptional cases.

1.4 Conquering Death

In the Puranic lore of the *Aryans*, there are three well-known cases where death was conquered. *Markandeya* was granted only sixteen years of life by the Lord himself. When his last moment arrived, he saw death face to face. By the Lord's grace earned by firm belief and deep prayer, the last moment of his life was halted or frozen and it never came to pass. He conquered death forever. But he conquered only his own death.

Savitri's husband, *Satyavan*, in her full view, slumped and succumbed to death. She saw the God of Death face to face, pulling *Satyavan* from out of his body with a rope. She saw the subtle body of her husband as the *Angusthamatra Purusha*, a one-inch-sized ethereal replica of his physical form. That the

Jivatman is verily the *Angustha Purusha* is evident from this episode which is also described in the *Devi Bhagavata* and the *Mahabharata*. She tried to stop the God of Death and argued with him for her husband's life. Thus, she conversed with the God of Death while she was in her own physical body, obviously through her Yogic-state.

Savitri, the boon child of her parents, alone could do this. She was granted three boons by the God of Death just as in the case of Nachiketa. All three boons related to worldly life. She was granted the boon of a son as her third boon. Once it was granted (inadvertently?) by the God of Death, her husband had to be restored to provide it for her. She won her claim by extraordinary willpower and God's grace. She saw death face to face, while she remained in her physical body without experiencing any separation from it. She conquered the death of her husband after he had actually died when his *Jivatman* departed. *Savitri's* feat is an extraordinary miracle because it conquered another person's death.

Sri Krishna performed yet another great feat. His teacher *Sandipani* had lost his son long ago. The boy's *Jivatman* was in the other world. *Krishna* brought him back into the physical body and restored his teacher back his own son. This is unthinkable even for a *Maha Yogi*. But *Sri Krishna* was God himself.

Nachiketa saw the God of Death after he had left his mortal body behind. He performed the rare feat of obtaining the secret of conquering death as a preamble to *Moksha* from the God of Death himself. This revelation was for the good of all mankind. Thus, he possibly conquered anyone's death. It behoves us to understand the significance of Nachiketa's achievement and investigate if there is any practical method delineated in this wonderful story.

It is noteworthy that death conquered elsewhere did not always involve a path to *Moksha*. Such a path, in the case of Nachiketa, was shown by the God of Death himself tacitly. For the sake of *Moksha*, therefore, the conquering of death has the approval of the Gods for everyone. Otherwise, the Law of Death is inexorable. Yoga is a science long known to the mankind and its assistance can be taken for this noble aim.

1.5 The Individual and his Continuity

What does conquering death imply?

The man who indulges in *Karma* is one personality, and the one who reaps its results is another due to the fact that death and rebirth, although of the same soul, have broken the continuity of his world experience. Hence, the average man is unable to comprehend the *Karma* — result relationship of his actions. The continuity of the soul in different incarnations has only to be experienced to know this deep secret of creation. By then, the mystery is not only solved but the ultimate threshold is open for the man for a permanent release from bondage.

Leaving the decrepit and useless physical body but continuing to be the same individual beyond the body thus avoiding the need to become a 'new individual' every birth. Such is the definition of conquering of death derived from this *Upanishad.* The individual is that aspect of the soul (*Asmita*) which identifies the soul with the body, which is the law of nature. This law of nature is responsible for owning the body and, nourishing it and all of its needs with great care so that the species can survive.

Survival of the species is required in order to provide the necessary bodies for all the souls awaiting the process of evolution from dark ignorance to pure knowledge and release from nature into the ultimate. A body is necessary for the experience of nature by every soul, thus leading to discrimination and wisdom and the onward march to the desire for release before it is finally absorbed. Billions of souls await such nature-experience, being steeped in ignorance of their real nature of purity. It is necessary for one to realise the futility of living in nature and also to conquer the power of nature over the soul by nurturing one's desire for release and by perpetuating the chosen path to reach it. The earlier path is, thus, continued.

But the law of nature working as death and rebirth strikes the soul in such a way that every time a new path is chosen, it meets the same fate of an abrupt end with death of the individual. With death, the mind and all its acquired knowledge gets destroyed. Thus, there is no continuity of the seeker or his chosen path. Even the desire to attain *Moksha* is often forgotten. This lapse must be overcome. For this reason, the individual — the soul with the same ego — must continue to exist and live beyond this body until the goal is attained. That is the requirement.

1.6 The Teacher-Disciple Tradition

There are various types of teachers as well as seekers. True teachers are those who have attained *Jnana* (knowledge) by their *Tapas* and are therefore competent to teach the way of Self-knowledge. A disciple pursues the path as a human being. For having shown the path, the disciple is indebted to the Guru and in his gratitude gives the Guru what all he can, as a proof of his surrender to him.

The Guru in this particular *Upanishad* is the God who controls the path of souls beyond their human bodies. The Guru here is not a mere teacher, but the giver of the path and its goal as well. Strangely, the Guru here seems to have become indebted to the disciple, paying his debt, as it were, for an omission in hospitality to the disciple. What did the disciple here do to deserve such a gift directly from this God? It was owing to Nachiketa's ability to reach the God of Death, without a body, yet without dying and patiently waiting for his *Darsan* (vision).

There was no more *Sadhana* involved beyond this point. By virtue of this great state and his strong desire to have the knowledge as well as liberation, Nachiketa received the gift directly. In such a state of being, the soul does not have to undertake any further practice or study but becomes instantly eligible for the secret key to liberation. Making him wait for three nights at his door became an apparent omission on the part of the Guru. The disciple has nothing to offer to the Guru, having already renounced everything in the mundane world. Nachiketa was at the end of his path and the teacher had no reason to delay in teaching him.

1.7 The Triple Sacrifice: *Visvajit*

The ancient Dharma ordained that one's wealth could be forfeited if a guest was made to wait long unattended. This law applied to the God Yama as well, when he left his young guest uncared for. The mystery remains as to what could be the wealth of this God? The wealth of the Gods is nothing but the offerings that humans have made to them.

In the *Visvajit* sacrifice (*Yaga*), Auddalaka, the father of Nachiketa, gave away all his cattle and also sacrificed his merit of the sacrifice in order to deserve *Moksha* (liberation) by implication. The third wealth to be sacrificed was his progeny namely his son, Nachiketa, for the *Veda* says:

Na karmanaa na prajayaa dhanena
Tyaagenaike amritatva maanasuh

Moksha is attained not by wealth, action (including meritorious actions) or even progeny, but only by sacrificing (renouncing these three things).

At the end of the *Visvajit Yaga*, Auddalaka had forgotten to give away his son. And so, Nachiketa reminded his father as to what he proposed to do with him (Nachiketa). It was only then that the sacrifice could be completed. Thus, Nachiketa completed the process of his father's earning eligibility for *Moksha*.

And where did these gifts that Auddalaka gave away go to? The essence of what is sacrificed on earth reaches the God in the higher world to which they are offered. The meritorious actions of men dedicated to the Gods form the wealth of the Gods, only to be given away by the Gods to men seeking it in prayer. This is earthy wealth. All such wealth accumulated with the God could be forfeited by one omission in serving a guest and the God corrected it by making amends as boons to the guest.

However, such wealth as sacrificed by his father was not what he sought. Nachiketa wanted the secret knowledge about the soul and the key to its redemption. This was the real boon he was after. Once he made this request, it had to be given to him.

The law of *Karma* with its results accruing to living being is inexorable. Men engage themselves in noble deeds of charity, which results in wealth to their progeny because men strongly desire their sons and daughters to be happy. Those who renounce their progeny have no way of reaping the results of such charity. In their case, desire of every kind is sacrificed, leaving no cause for rebirth.

1.8 Yama as the Guru and Benefactor

There is a tradition in which certain Gods acted as Gurus like *Varuna Deva* teaching *Bhrigu*, the path of gradual realisation, which forms the text of *Bhriguvalli* in the *Taittiriya Upanishad.* But this incident of Nachiketa was unprecedented as it involved Yama, the God of Death. Gods like Yama and *Varuna*, being inseparable parts of Almighty God, are capable of granting direct knowledge as a boon without even necessarily showing the path. Paths, teaching and *Sadhana* are all earthly phenomenon. *Agni*, who is worshipped in the *Yaagas* could himself give such a *Jnana* to humans as well.

1.9 The Philosophy Involved

This *Upanishad* indicates the apparent duality of *Jivatman* and *Paramatman* at one stage and their oneness in the state of realisation. In the state of duality, the all-pervasive *Paramatman* is witness to the experiences of the individualised soul. The *Upanishad* sounds dualistic at one point and ends on a note of *Advaita* or non-duality when *Moksha* is described.

2. BACKGROUND OF THE *UPANISHAD*: *YAJNA*, *TAPAS* AND *YOGA*

2.1 *Yajna* and Sacrifice

Nachiketa belonged to the great *Gautama Gotra* or family of Rishis, one of the seven main Rishi lines. *Gautama Muni* was a well-known sage even before *Ramayana* times. It could have been during *Ramayana* times or a little later that this episode of Nachiketa took place. This was a time in which the four-fold demarcation of the *Vedas* (*Samhitas*, *Brahmanas*, *Aranyakas* and *Upanishads)* may not have provided clarity to the common people about the various levels of Vedic thought relative to the ritual and its spiritual import. Among the more learned sections of Aryan society, however, it is reasonable to assume that the ritual was accompanied by knowledge of its philosophical import, the core principle behind it.

Although the ritual had a meticulous detail to be scrupulously observed by its performer, not everyone understood its spiritual significance. Nevertheless, the results of such rituals would be achieved in the course of time as a consequential reward. The story of Nachiketa is a visible commentary on the import of Vedic rituals like the *Visvajit Yaga*. For the attainment of the higher worlds promised in the ritual, the sacrifice of one's wealth here on earth was imperative.

Further, the priests or Brahmins who assisted in the *Yajna* had to be paid sumptuously, because such liberal payment involves the spirit of sacrifice in the performer of the *Yajna*. If, all that one had was given away at the performance of a *Yaga* like the *Visvajit*, it resulted in many spiritual benefits both here and now and in the life beyond.

But without understanding its merit and without having a spirit of sacrifice, a *Yajna* was considered lifeless and capable of giving only very limited benefits. The *Yajna* also required a precise knowledge of the meticulous formalities to be observed in its performance. A thorough understanding of the *Brahmana* and *Aranyaka* was an unavoidable qualification for a good *Yajna*, in addition to finding learned Brahmin helpers. For this reason, the performance of a *Yajna,* both true in spirit and perfect in practice was not easy or within the reach of everyone.

The difficulty in the proper performance of *Yajnas* led to the emergence of other easier but equally efficacious paths for the attainment of higher worlds like *Svarga*. These were devotion to God, wisdom, renunciation, spiritual practice (Yoga) and *Tapas*. In these paths of later ages, Vedic rituals became gradually less important and these paths became more universal, crossing the barriers of caste-*brahminical* eligibilities, a situation reached even during the *Mahabharata* times. Later, the attainment of higher worlds through Vedic rituals became less attractive and less significant in the *Aryan* culture than the goal of *Moksha*. Since no caste superiority was related or considered relevant to the path of *Jnana* (knowledge) that led to *Moksha*, the ritualism that was restricted to the eligible upper caste *Aryans* naturally faded in importance. A thorough understanding of the *Brahmana* and *Aranyaka* was an unavoidable qualification for a good *Yagna* in addition to finding learned Brahmin helpers.

2.2 Spirituality and Sacrifice

In the course of Vedic culture in post-Buddhist and post-*Sankara* times, the ritual became declared as irrelevant to the path of *Moksha*. Even the theory of '*Karma jnana Samutchaya*', which argued that *Karma* or the 'Vedic ritual path' could be followed with a spiritual attitude to achieve liberation, was rejected by the followers of the '*Jnana* path' on the rationale that such *Karma* is neither *Jnana*-based nor *Jnana*-yielding.

But if we go back to the earlier times in Aryan history, we find that *Moksha* was once considered by some to be the fruit of Karma accompanied by *Jnana*. The *Jnana* here propounded was knowledge of the pure spirit behind the creation, and also of the pervading qualified spirit in the creation called '*Prajapati*' (the one God in the *jivas*).

The attempt was more to dissolve one's own qualified existence into *Prajapati*, denuding the self within of all conditioning, leaving it to ultimately merge in the unqualified *Brahman*. The *Asvamedha* (horse sacrifice), in fact, was considered as one such ritual leading to dissolution or *Moksha*.

It is in relation to the spiritual significance of a well done Vedic sacrifice that this *Upanishad* should be studied. The *Upanishad* starts with the *Visvajit* sacrifice of Auddalaka and ends with renunciation of the benefits of another sacrifice that came into existence from a boon granted by Yama to Nachiketa. From the *Visvajit Yajna*, it has to be inferred that Nachiketa's father, Auddalaka* had already attained a great power of the Word. By his mere utterance, Auddalaka granted his son an experience of death without death actually occurring. This experience of death helped Nachiketa unravel the mystery of death. The prescription of the '*Nachiketa Yajna*' by Yama, named after the boy, could grant a long and fruitful life on earth, a higher world as desired by the performer, and ultimate salvation through meditation on *Pranava (Om)*.

Such a wonderful ritual was unprecedented, like the experience of death by Nachiketa itself was. This ritual of the

**In this regard we should note that Uddalaka Aruni and his son Svetaketu, from whom the name of Nachiketa's father as Auddalaka arose, are also important figures in the* Chandogya Upanishad, *connecting them to these great teachers.*

Nachiketa Yajna is not very elaborate when compared to others like the Visvajit, but it additionally demands knowledge of Yoga along with a strong desire for liberation. Among the Brahmins of those times were two different groups; one took to a life in the forest, with minimum rituals but dedicated to the practice of Tapas or internal purification and meditational practices. The other lived with the people in the villages and was obliged to perform Vedic sacrifices both for themselves and for others. They needed to learn the importance of spiritual goals in rituals, which were more important than the material benefits involved. The incident of Nachiketa, perhaps, fulfilled such a purpose.

2.3 Yajna and Tapas

This *Upanishad* shows the relevance of the Vedic *Yajna* to the path of renunciation, *Tapas* and the attainment of *Moksha*, thus clearing the minds of those, who look upon such ritualism as irrelevant to the spiritual path. It serves as a bridge between ritualism and spirituality. This truth has been specifically stated in the *Upanishad* (Valli-3, Mantra-2) itself.

The descent of the *Vedas* to earth was possible solely due to *Tapas*. In the Vedic view the entire universe comes into being through *Tapas*. The goal of *Tapas*, therefore, has necessarily to be 'knowledge'. There can be no *Tapas* without a goal. The revelation of the *Vedas* to those who meditated was the fulfillment of their *Tapas*. The enormous size of the *Vedas* reflects a great amount of *Tapas* performed by numerous sages in the past. The *Vedas*, therefore, are capable of growing endlessly, if there is continuing *Tapas*. The statement of '*Anantaa vai Vedaah*' or 'unlimited are the *Vedas*' points to this. For the same reason, the *Vedas* could be lost if the practice of *Tapas* was discontinued. Thus over a time the practice of the Vedic ritual and study of the *Vedas* was neglected. What we see today in Aryan culture is a result of this. Perfection of the ritual and the deeper knowledge that it supported has gone into a severe decline as well.

However, a new phenomenon known as 'Yoga' came into existence as a development of the inner aspect of the sacrifice when the sacrifice declined.*

2.4 The True *Yajna* and its Decline

At one time, a very major Vedic sacrifice like *Asvamedha* was clearly understood to be a Vedic ritual with a spiritual goal and being a means to attain the higher worlds. We have long drifted away from this. Unless the ash-covered embers of spirituality are stoked, together with a combined study of the Upanishads and the *Brahmanas* that deal with the spirit behind the rituals, this great secret culture is soon bound to completely die. A casual reading and inept handling of Yoga practices here and there is not enough for us to appreciate this practical science that can render great service to mankind even today.

Literature on Yoga may make interesting if not curious reading for the commoner but it does not lead anywhere without serious practice. Such literature in itself is not capable of playing any vital role in the revival of the most valuable part of the Aryan culture — the *Tapas,* through which much good can be achieved both for oneself and for mankind.

Commentaries on *Upanishads* appear in public even today. However, mere intellectual discussion on the abstruse topics of Vedanta and subjects like *Moksha* and *Brahman* can do little beyond entertaining the reader, if they don't evoke a

*This is a meditational practice for one's own spiritual benefit. It is a modern version of the ancient *Tapas* suited for the materialistic life of today and the limited capacities of modern man. Yet even this lesser substitute for the ancient Tapas is poorly practised in modern society, in which the desire for an inner experience of spirit or *Moksha* has become a rarity. It is, however, significant to note that this culture is not totally dead but very much alive in various places in Hindu and even in non-Hindu society, though seekers today are facing the powerful challenges of materialism. It is, therefore, necessary that we explore what the ancient spiritual and ritualistic literature has to tell us about it.

practical interest in the attainment of the spiritual goal. But performance of *Tapas* cannot form the activity of a community or be done en masse because it is highly personal and individualistic. However, revelation of the secrets contained in the Vedic lore of the *Upanishads* and *Brahmanas* may lead one to a practical involvement in *Tapas*, when stories like that of Nachiketa are retold and taken to heart.

In producing a new literature on Yoga, we seem to be slowly drifting away from the main body of the *Vedas*, *Brahmanas*, *Aranyakas* and *Upanishads*. It is, therefore necessary to acquaint people with this Vedic spiritual-lore while teaching Yoga. More importantly, specialised hermitages with competent teaching and training only can benefit serious seekers who are not content with mere discourse but wish to engage in the deeper practices.

2.5 *Vedanta* and *Sadhana*

Another significant trend of Vedantic literature in India today is philosophical sectarianism. For every work on *Advaita* published, it seems inevitable that two more works on *Dvaita* and *Visistaadvaita* must be written in order to counter it. These medieval born theoretical systems within today's Hinduism are keen on propagating their respective philosophies in opposition to one another.

2.6 Medieval and Modern Society

In the more than twelve centuries since *Sri Sankara* expounded his profound *Advaita* philosophy, establishing it as the essence of the trinity of our original texts, the *Brahma Sutras*, *Upanishads* and *Bhagavadgita*, there has been a spate of argumentative expositions by scholars for or against the theory of *Advaita*. All such literature is certainly a treat for the well-educated intellectual who is eager to know the theory about the Ultimate Truth, the nature of God and so on. But to the common man in Hindu society today, who is seeking guidance for spiritual practice, these abstruse philosophies of monism or dualism are like Greek or Latin.

What he is badly in need of is either a practical guide to genuine ancient paths of spiritual practice or a basic education in commonplace Hindu religious practices. For him, the mutually disagreeing and condemning philosophical doctrines, the *Upanishadic* literature, or the manuals of elaborate ritualism do not have any significance or yield any attraction. Commonplace and simple Hindu methods of worship, a devotional path in life and a revival of temple culture in society are what is required to satisfy the needs of most people today. The phenomenon of Hinduism is too complex and too big to be epitomised. The unattractive controversial literature on pure philosophy and the schisms in society caused by the advocates of exclusive forms of God are certainly not conducive to the unification of Hindu society. The bulk of Hindu society has been following a wide variety of saints for over a millennium now, ranging from figures of national repute to locally inspiring personalities whose influence is more on the morals, faith and devotion and sometimes, involves more the worship of the saints themselves than even of God. The philosophies have little significance to such people who are preoccupied with pilgrimages and temples. The result is that the range and variety of paths is ever widening, defying any standard classification.

2.7 *Advaita* and Duality

In the course of establishing *Advaita*, *Sankara* refuted *Sankhya-related* Yoga Siddhanta, countering its assertion that the *Jivas* or souls are not one with Isvara or God. Advaita has ever since occupied the centre stage in Hindu theology and Yoga as a science or as a philosophy was reduced to insignificance. The ten important Upanishads have, as a rule, been repeatedly commented upon in order to elicit an *Advaitic* assertion.

However, there are *Upanishadic* assertions which can be interpreted as indicating the duality of *Jiva* and *Isvara*, though both being one and the same in origin and dissolution. We may therefore treat all the systems of philosophy as true contextually, being complimentary as a sequence. Yoga as a practical attempt to gain the experience of the Self in its bound as well as released states can therefore provide a common path or bridge between dualistic and monistic theories.

2.8 This Humble Attempt

Keeping these hard facts in view, this *Upanishad* has been commented upon here not on the '*Purvapaksha Siddhanta*' (hypothesis-criticism-assertion) model in the support of either monism or dualism, but with a view to bring out only the spiritual emphasis of the *Upanishad* relative to the inner practice called Yoga. It is hoped that reading this interpretation will provide a fresh look at the *Upanishad*, which has been profusely commented upon by various learned scholars from *Adi Sankara* till today. Most of these have treated the *Upanishad* as conveying the *Advaitic* message alone, which undoubtedly is true but only as its goal.

The nature-soul (*Purusha-Prakriti*) combination according to *Sankhya* results in intellect (*Buddhi*), self-consciousness (*Ahamkara*) and the other *tattvas*. The soul, which is the experiencer of nature, seeks final bliss, which is freedom from nature. This bliss results from discrimination (*viveka*) between nature and the soul, without confusion. The very tendency of the soul to seek bliss is its inherent virtue. The arising intellect and functions of consciousness are tools of the soul for *Sadhana* until nature finally leaves the soul. This process of seeking the bliss of freedom from nature is expounded as the practice of Yoga.

The *Sruti* says, '*Aatmaavaare drastavyah srotavyo mantavyo nidhidhyaasitavyah*' meaning that 'the Self alone is to be seen, heard, thought about and meditated on'. This statement establishes the need and efficacy of a deliberate process to achieve the goal. For this process the grace of *Isvara*, who is defined in Yoga as *Om* or *Pranava* (*Tasya Vaachakah Pranavah*, *Yoga Sutras*), is to be depended upon.

The details of the practice involve different stages variously described as *chakras*, *mantras* and deities according to the methods of the *Yoga Sastra.* All these stages are of temporary importance that ultimately lead to the dissolution of the soul in the *Paramatman* in the heart-centre after all qualified conditioning of consciousness is dropped behind.

The *Purva Mimamsa* or ritualistic school of Jaimini, on the other hand, does not take God into account, not even as the author of the *Veda*, which it regards as self-revealing and eternal and hence an infallible authority in its own right. Even the deities to whom the sacrifice is offered do not yield their rewards by any power of theirs. It is the power of the ritual itself, known as '*Apurva*' which alone can do this. The path of sacrifice therefore, is capable of, in the ultimate sense, destroying the Karma of both merit and demerit, resulting in freedom from bondage. But the most important ingredient of Karma in such sacrifices is non-attachment to the fruit of action.

The Katha Upanishad, in its unique approach, takes the help of the power of sacrifice (*Nachiketa Agni* etc.) from *Purva Mimamsa*; the power of God through the meditation on the various deities and the *Mantras* in the *Chakras* (who are only components of the One almighty God), and the basic theory of *Sankhya* while defining the factors that cause the soul to be bound. In this wonderful blending, it establishes the ultimate goal of the soul as merging with the *Brahman* or *Paramatman* in the heart-centre. The apparent conflicts between these different systems or *Darsanas*, thus, cease to exist.

The experience of death is the most significant new ingredient in this *Upanishad.* It is used to show that the soul's independence and separateness from the body it occupies. This has to be experienced without death itself actually occurring. This state of getting out of the body or leaving the body behind, with half of the life-force left in it, while taking the other half along with it by the soul, is shown to benefit the soul with a direct perception of reality. This is quite different from a mere intellectual conviction about the soul in essence being different from the body obtained by a discussion and analysis of the philosophy of the texts.

The *Upanishad* tells us that such a direct perception of the independence of the soul results in conquering death forever. A helpless death is a painful process of separating from the body as the law of nature works in all living creatures. This helps one to the direct realisation of the absolute truth by taking refuge in the meditation on *Om*.

3. THE EPISODE OF NACHIKETA

3.1 The Episode — a Further Examination

Auddalaka Aruni was a great sage who spent his long life in the performance of *Tapas*. He eventually performed a sacrifice known as *Visvajit*, meaning 'the conquering of the world'. He gave away all his wealth in charity. The young Nachiketa, his son, goaded by a strange doubt from within, disturbed his father three times with the question, "Father, to whom will you give me away?" Goaded by destiny again, the father blurted, "To Death, you shall be given!" The power of the Tapas of the sage made these words of his a reality.

However, Nachiketa was not ordered to die physically. Nachiketa, not having died as a human being, only left his body but he continued on as an individual. In death, the individual dies and the soul has no means of recognising anyone like the God of Death, since it has lost its consciousness. As an individual not dying but leaving his body, Nachiketa remembered the words of his father. He, therefore, looked forward to be received by the God of Death, which is a state of meditation. Such an intention enabled him to see the God of Death without getting lost in the abysmal darkness of death. This *Upanishad* proves that such a state is possible in which a soul can continue as an individual beyond the body or go out of its body without dying - leaving the body temporarily behind with life but no soul. It also proves that an individual soul can travel as he wishes outside the body, if there is a premeditated *Sankalpa* and yogic power to do this.

Nachiketa is said to have waited three nights for the appearance of Yama, the God of Death, who on seeing him seemingly regretted not having attended on him. "Oh Nachiketa, what did you eat these three nights?" the God of Death asked. Nachiketa replied, "on the first night, I consumed your progeny; on the second night, your cattle wealth and on the third night, your merit (*punya*)." The God claimed his wealth back in exchange for the three boons granted to Nachiketa like going back to his father on earth, a life of earthly prosperity and happiness etc. Nachiketa then, sought from Yama, the secret knowledge of the phenomenon of the souls transiting the worlds like earth to heaven etc. After insistence by Nachiketa, he revealed to him the secret, tacitly, appreciating his firmness in his great desire. Yama taught him a secret ritual for conquering death, together with its secret principles. He also taught him the path of liberation.

This story at the outset obviously raises many questions; such as; Did Nachiketa go to the house of Death with his body? Why was not the God seen immediately, but only after a lapse of three nights? What is meant by Nachiketa going without food for three nights? What is meant by 'the wealth of progeny, cattle and merit of the God', being destroyed?

We have already answered the first question with our view that Nachiketa did not go with his physical body. The three nights of waiting, obviously, was the Tapas required before having a vision of the God-Guru. After all, Tapas has to be ultimately defined as — keen waiting for the ultimate experience with *Sraddha* or devotion for the object sought, faith in the achievement and total trust in the Giver's grace. These were possible for Nachiketa because he was beyond his bodily limitations, which included a 'material body-consciousness' replaced by 'self-consciousness' as well as freedom from hunger and sleep that go with the physical body. The threatened loss of the wealth of the God-Guru indicates how the God or Guru has no freedom not to give what is sought by an eminently eligible disciple.

Nachiketa Agni is the name given to the ritual taught by Yama. If it resulted in the attainment of the heaven, what was its specialty since there were many other rituals resulting in heaven? If the path to liberation was granted and explained, what was so new about it? An attempt should be made to know answers to these questions.

3.2 The ingredients of the *Upanishad*: The relevant *Brahmana, Visvajit* Yaga:

Sacrificing one's possessions for *Moksha*

Apart from the *Upanishad*, the concerned *Brahmana* portion of this *Veda* states:

Usanhavai Vaajasravasah sarvavedasam dadau
Tasya ha Nachiketaa naama putra aasa
Tagm ha kumaaragm santam
Dakshinaasu neeyamaanaasu sraddhaavivesa, Sa ho vaacha
Tata kasmai maam daasyaseeti dviteeyam triteeyam

(Taittiriya Brahmana, 3.11.8)

Auddalaka gave away all his possessions as a *Dakshina* (charitable gift) on the fifth day ritual of the *Visvajit Yaga* (known as *Madhyandina savanam*). The injunction of the Sastra is that all one's possessions must be given away. The injunction is *Sarvasvam dadaati*. The word *Sarvasvam* has been interpreted by some to include one's father, mother and son also. The *Purva Mimamsa* of Jaimini (VI.7.1) contains some Sutras in which the *Visvajit Yaga* has been discussed. The above interpretation that "all possessions" include father, mother and son has been rejected saying that one was not a master of these three because they are not part of his possessions.

In the third *Sutra* of the second *Adhikarana*, it was argued that one's own land also should not be given away as charity. The argument is that the land belongs to no one exclusively and all creatures have a right over it. The man owning the land has a right only on the crops that are growing on it but not the land itself, which is a permanent thing. In the fourth *Sutra* of third *Adhikarana*, even the horses one possessed are forbidden from being given away, for no one should accept as charity animals having both upper and lower teeth. In the sixth *Sutra* of fifth *Adhikarana*, it has been forbidden to give away in charity one's own *Sudra* (servant) or one who is serving him for (seeking) education etc. In *Sutra-7* of *Adhikarana*-6, it has been concluded that one should give away all other wealth that he has in his possession like money, at the time of the *Yaga Dakshina* being offered. In *Sutra-14* of *Adhikarana-8*, the matter has been further discussed and decided that in the *Visvajit Yaga*, performed as part of *Ahargana Astaratra Yaga*, one should give away all the money at his disposal. (In this eight-night ritual, the first day ritual is *Visvajit* and the last day's ritual is known as *Abhijit*). In the *Jyotistoma* sacrifice, 112 coins of standard denomination have been prescribed. The famous scholar Kumarila Bhatta has held that in the *Visvajit* Yaga a similar amount must be given.

In the story of Nachiketa, Auddalaka gave his son Nachiketa away to the God of Death deliberately, which lead to a dangerous situation. It appears that keeping this incident in view the *Purva Mimamsa* took it up for discussion and the propriety of giving away one's son, horse or land was considered on individual merits. At the time when such propriety was not considered, Nachiketa considered himself as part of his father's wealth, and genuinely asked his father as to whom he himself should be given away.

Tagm ha pareeta uvaacha mrityave tvaa dadaameeti

"I give you to Death", he said, in anger.

Tagm ha smotthitam vaagabhivadati
Gautamakumaara miti
Sa ho vaacha parehi mrityoh grihaan
Mrityave vai tva adaamiti

On hearing his father's words, Nachiketa moved aside from his father. Then a voice from the sky addressed him thus: "Oh *Gautama*! Your father has truly said that he would give you away to Death."

Tam vai pravasantam gantaaseeti ho vaacha
Tasyasma tisroraatreeh anasnan grihe vasataat
Sa yaditvaa prichhet
Kumaara kati raatreeh avaatseeriti? Tisra iti pratibrootaat
Kim prathamaagm raatrimaasnaa iti? Prajaan ta iti
Kim dviteeyaamiti? Pasoogmsta iti
Kim triteeyaamiti? Saadhu krityaanta iti

The voice from the sky continued: "Oh Nachiketa! When you go to the house of Death in accordance with your father's orders, Yama, the God of Death, will be away. Stay in his house three nights without taking any food. On his return, Yama will ask you, "Son! How many nights have you stayed in my house?" Answer that you stayed there for three nights. "What did you eat the first night?" He will ask you. "I consumed your progeny," you should say. "What did you eat the second night?" He will ask you. "I consumed your cattle," you should say. "What did you eat the third night?" He will ask you. "I consumed your merit," should be your reply.

3.3 Nachiketa's Experience: Some Questions

Nachiketa as instructed by the *Akasa Vani* or voice from the sky (obviously an inner voice) reached the home of God of Death when he was away and stayed for three nights without food. Upon his arrival home, the God Yama questioned Nachiketa in the predicted manner. Nachiketa replied as advised by the voice from the sky earlier.

How could the God be away from his home? It means the *Jivatman* remained bodiless and took three days to have the Darsan of the God. On leaving the human body, the *Jivatman* would obviously go without food and water for some days and nights and eventually forget the habit of taking them. For a person sitting in *Dhyana* nearly suspending his breath, it usually takes three years to get rid of the habit of taking food and water on earth. The three days and nights of Nachiketa without a body are of a terrestrial duration. In this case, due to the instructions from the sky received in advance, Nachiketa left this world with such a resolve (*Sankalpa*).

What is meant by consuming the possessions of a householder even like the God of Death? It is a *Dharmic* law of this world that if food and water are expected by a visitor and not given to him, it results in forfeiture of the householder's possessions. For a soul that has departed from the body, food and water are offered by his responsible survivors on earth. It is also followed by *Tarpana* (special water oblations). Without them the soul would experience a condition of hunger and thirst in the after-death state.

We had earlier noticed that Nachiketa did not die but his individual soul left behind a body with life. This is obvious because he later returned to his father's home on earth by virtue of another boon given by Yama. The body in the father's home was alive without a soul in it. This phenomenon is possible through Yoga (to be explained later). For this reason, his father had not offered any food, water or oblations to his departed son. Thus, on earth too Nachiketa did not receive any food or water, though he had reached a place where such food and water could be expected. This is a lesson in Dharma for us.

Namaste astu bhagava iti hovaacha
Varam vrineeshveti
Pitarameva jivannayaaneeti

Yama said to Nachiketa: 'Salutations to you. Ask for a boon'. Nachiketa requested him that he should come to life and return to his father.

Dviteeyam vrineeshveti
Istaapoortayorme akshitim brooheeti hovaacha
Tasmai haitamagnim Naachiketamuvaacha
Tato vai tasyeshtaapoorte naaksheeyete

Nachiketa requested for perpetual fulfillment of *Istapurtas*, i.e., performance of Vedic rituals and sacrifices (Ista) and undertaking works of public utility, such as planting trees, digging of wells, constructing tanks etc., (Purta). The God granted his desires and said that by the performance of certain *Agnichayana*, a ritual known as *Nachiketa Agni*, the results of many other rituals could also be achieved.

Naasyeshtaapoorte ksheeyete
Yo agnim Naachiketam chinute
Ya u chainam evam veda

By knowledge of the secret of the performance of *Nachiketa Agni*, such benefits would become perpetual.

Triteeyam vrineeshveti
Punarmrityorme pachitim brooheeti hovaacha
Tasmai haitamagnim Naachiketamuvaacha
Tatovai so apapunarmrityum ajayat
Apapunarmrityum jayati
Yo agnim Naachiketam chinute
Ya u chainam evam veda

"Ask for the third boon," Yama said. "When I die in this body, I reach another body only to die again. If I am not reborn, (another) death is conquered. Tell me the way for such attainment."

The God explained to him the details of Nachiketa Agni along with its principles and practice. Mere ritual without Upasana (meditation) could grant all material desires on earth, but meditation on its spirit as Upasana following the performance of Nachiketa Agni would enable one to conquer rebirth as well. Mere performance of the ritual is insufficient for conquering death or for the still higher goal of liberation. Thus, the ritual is secondary in importance when the higher goal is kept in mind. The God's intention is that Upasana or meditation on the principle and concept should accompany the performance of the ritual. This brings us to the appreciation of the importance of Antaryaaga or the inner psychic ritual such as meditation as the more significant part of Vedic rituals. The importance of the inner ritual has been traditionally stressed elsewhere as well.

4. THE SUBTLE BODY AND THE SELF WITHIN THE HEART

4.1 *Linga Sarira*: The 'Individual' Soul

The *Yoga Sastra* accepts the axioms of the *Sankhya* system that the *Jivas* are many, different from *Isvara* and that in a body the *Jivatman* is the *Purusha* or enjoyer of *Prakriti*. This *Jivatman* even in the *Upanishads*, which are the basis of Vedanta, is referred to as the *Angustha Purusha* or the *Purusha* the size of a thumb. Elsewhere in the *Upanishads* this *Jivatman* is referred to as the *linga sarira*. By a reference to *Sankhya* we will find that this is the same as the subtle body (*sukshma sarira)*. This *linga Sarira* consists of the ego, the mind, the five senses, the five elements in the subtle state and the five *Tanmatras - sabda*, *sparsa*, *roopa*, *rasa*, *gandha* - the sense objects of sound, touch, sight, taste and smell. This combination is the result of the Jiva's contact and complete identification with a physical body.

It is to be remembered that the *Paramatman* is the core inside the ethereal thumb sized reflection of a gross body. Hence, the meditation by the Jiva's *buddhi* on the *Paramatman* can lead to the vision and experience of the *Paramatman* inside the impermanent *Angustha Purusha*. Thus, the *Paramatman* is with the heart-centre. *Isvarah Sarvabhutanam Hriddese Arjuna Tishtati* (Bhagavadgita, 18-61). This may be taken to mean the governor of the past and future reincarnations. A Yogi who has realized this master within attains *Vibhutva* i.e., the all-pervasive ability. Such a Yogi can by deliberate *Sankalpa* be reborn for a purpose or live or assume more than one body at any time.

In the case of animal life, the *Jiva* within is unaware of his existence as an entity and lives only by instinct without *Manas*, *Buddhi*, *Ahamkara* and *Asmita*. Thus, only the human body is the starting point for self-awareness.

Isana, the supreme lord being present inside the *Jivatman* enables the *Jivatman* to carry the *Samskaras* within itself, even when the subtle body loses its shape during its existence between two bodies. This *linga sarira*, when it attains *Atma Jnana* or Self-knowledge, dissolves into *Prakriti*. This innermost truth, is the witness to the soul's complete journey through *Prakriti* or nature.

Sankhya philosophy's assertion of a multiplicity of *Jivas* and *Pradhana* or *Prakriti* as the ultimate origin of creation had been refuted by the *Advaita Sastra*. This and the subtle difference between the *Avyakta* (unmanifest) of the Vedantin and *Pradhana*, if any, do not affect the ability of Yoga to function as a means to *Moksha*. This is so because Yoga has taken the help of God in addition to the numerical components of creation and started with the bound-state of the *Jiva*. Even the *Brahma Sutras* (1.11) say, '*Guhaam pravishtau aatmaanau hi taddarsanaat*'. This means that the *Jivatman* has as its witness the *Paramatman* inside the heart-centre. This duality then ceases to affect *Jiva's* ability to realise the *Paramatman*.

Normally, the *linga sarira* retains the physical features of the lost physical body for some time after death. The *Mahabharata*, *Asramavasa Parva*, second chapter, contains an episode to this effect. The wives of the *Kauravas* and other heroes killed in the War attended *Vyasa's* hermitage on the *Ganga* where oblations and the necessary obsequies were offered to the departed. *Vyasa* offered a boon to the widowed women to show them their departed husbands that same night. He also offered them the option, if they desired to accompany their husbands to the higher world of happiness, which they earned by dying on the battlefield. Most of the women chose to leave this world and go with their husbands.

After nightfall, *Vyasa*, by the power of his *Tapas*, called the departed *Kauravas* etc. to come out from the *Ganga* with their bodies to meet their wives. The *Kauravas* and other warriors emerged from the *Ganga* with their spiritual or ethereal bodies in an excellent, happy condition with no traces of sorrow or hatred. The wives met their husbands that night and by their own will accompanied them back into the *Ganga*, from where those souls departed this world. This miracle was possible because the *linga Sariras* of the *Kauravas* still had the shape of their earthly bodies. The *Jivatman* continues to reside in the *linga sarira* with the shape of its former body until it leaves the atmosphere of earth to reach *Pitruloka* or other worlds. The wife accompanying the husband to the other world by choice is a very ancient practice known as '*Sahagamanam*'. Obviously, this is the companionship they would achieve beyond physical existence.

Once also in the distant past, the Rishi Vasistha and King Nimi cursed each other to lose their physical bodies. Vasistha, by virtue of his *Yogasakti*, even without his body – as a *linga sarira* – journeyed to the *Brahma Loka* and went round the God *Brahma*, praying for a new physical body, which was then granted to him. By *Brahma's* boon, he acquired a new body as a combination of the spiritual prowess of the two gods, *Mitra* and *Varuna*.

This *linga sarira*, by virtue of its own ego and mind, by meditation on V*ishnu*, *Siva* or other Gods, while in human body, can assume the shape of the deity of its concentration. This is the *Sarupya* attainment that liberates the soul from human births.

4.2 The Secret of the *Angustha Purusha*

What makes the *Atman* an individual in the body is none else than the existence of an entity called the *Angustha Purusha*, which means the person who is of the size of the thumb. Because of his miniature size we can call him the 'inch-man'. This inch-man does not contain the material of the physical body, as he is only ethereal. **He is an exact miniature of the physical body holding the same relative proportions.** Every movement and posture of the physical body is replicated in this model man. He is the soul with its aura and forms the core of the human individual.

The real experiencer of the body consciousness is, therefore, the *Angustha Purusha.* He receives all the sensations of the physical body and reacts physically and appropriately to them. A thorn in the foot of the man causes pain in the foot of the *Angustha Purusha.* This inch-man is the *Jivatman* or *Jiva.* His existence in the body is governed by the streams of life force, pervading the entire body starting from the heart-centre. From a point close to the heart-centre down to the *Muladhara chakra*, or sacro-coccygeal Yogic centre of the body, is the region in which the inch-man normally lives during the life-time of the body. He sustains by the alternating respirational dynamism of the *Ida* and *Pingala Nadis* or streams of life-energy. The *Purusha Sukta* describes him as:

Sa bhoomim visvato vritvaa atya tisthat dasaangulam
Purusha ye vedagm sarvam yadbhootam yatcha bhavyam
Utaamritatvasyaesaanah ...

Having encompassed the world on all sides (in *Muladhara*), he stands ten measures (inches) beyond (in heart centre). The *Purusha* is one who knows what has been and what will be and he presides over immortality.

This *Jivatman* in its true primordial state is none other than the *Paramatman* Himself. *Advaita Vedanta* asserts that *Avidya*, *Maya* or ignorance reflecting in pure *Brahman* is God or *Isvara* and *Isvara's* reflection in *Prakriti* (nature) is *Jiva.* Thus, *Isvara* or God must also be present within the human body, but where exactly? This *Isvara* or *Paramatman* **is present in the heart of the *Jiva* as a point with a bright aura that reflects in it the shape of the physical body as a miniature of its proportions.**

This supreme entity, endowed with life-energy acquiring a body-consciousness (*Chitta*), is working as the *Jivatman*. Thus, the *Paramatman* is surrounded by an ethereal body-reflection and endowed with a limited consciousness, in the man. This *Paramatman* is a 'dimensionless dot' of light within the *Jiva*, in its heart-centre. His effulgent presence enables the *Jivatman* to function in the body. For this reason, the *Angustha Purusha* is very often described as the *Paramatman* himself, while other times as the inner *Atman* or *Paramatman* or *Pratyagatman*. **Thus, the inner *Paramatman* is the true reality and *Jivatman* is but a relative, fleeting, impermanent and dependent reality.** Therefore, that 'One *Paramatman*' reflects Himself in all living bodies in their respective shapes accompanied by their respective egos and their accompanying body-consciousnesses. HE is an enduring all-time truth, meaning that HE is deathless and changeless.

To whom then, is the death that is referred to applies in this world? As we have seen, the physical body is reflected in all its proportions in the ethereal (subtle or astral) body. Therefore, the destruction of the physical body will eventually destroy the inch-sized shape of the ethereal body also over a time. Having lost its ethereal shape, the core soul alone remains as a 'dot indestructible', unaffected by life or death but surrounded by a shapeless aura containing the impurities of tendencies or *Samskaras* acquired in previous birth, waiting for reincarnation in the next human body. It is a deathless entity.

A discussion of the *Kosas* that enwrap the soul is relevant here.

4.3 The Five Sheaths

The Taittiriya Aranyaka (10.71) says —
Angusthamaatrah purusho Angusthamcha samaasritah
Esassarvasya jagatah prabhuh preenaati visvabhuk

The *Purusha* the size of the thumb, as well as HE who dwells therein is the Lord ruling the entire world and is 'experiencing' the world also.

The *Angustha Purusha* contains *Isvara*, the Lord of Creation. The *Taittiriya Upanishad* describes the five sheaths of the body assumed by the *linga Sarira* or *Jivatman*. Next to the physical gross body, its replica, similar in shape is the *Annamaya Kosa*.

Similar to this in shape, the next subtle body is *Pranamaya Kosa*. This consists of the respiration or the life function as its essence. In this subtle body, *Prana* exists as wind. It is here called the *Samana*. Since we know *Samana Prana* is situated near the navel region, the *Pranamaya Sarira* has its centre there. The man, who meditates on this *Pranamaya Sarira*, concentrating his thought that he is *Prana* himself, acquires a very long life in his physical body.

The next subtler body inside this *Pranamaya Kosa*, similar in shape, is *Manomaya Kosa*. The *Sruti* describes that the *Vedas* are its head, the *Brahmana* (portion of the *Vedas*) is its *Atman* and the *Atharva Aangirasa mantras* form its basis. This is to say that this body has for its content, the Vedic intellectual knowledge.

The next subtler body inside the *Manomaya* is the *Vijnanamaya Kosa*. *Sraddha* is its head, *Rtam* and *Satyam* are its sides, and Yoga is its resting-place (*Samadhana*). This subtle body is the plane of consciousness for *Tapas* or Yoga. One who meditates on it, assuming it to be *Brahman*, destroys all his sins and fulfils all his desires. Let us understand that this is the condition of living of the higher divine beings like *Devas* and *Gandharvas* etc.

Finally, the subtlest and innermost sheath inside *Vijnanamaya Kosa* is *Anandamaya Kosa*, which too has the human shape. The *Sruti* says, *Priyam* is its head, *Moda* and *Pramoda* are its right and left sides and *Ananda* (bliss) is its soul. *Priyam* is to be understood as the thought or vision of the desired object. *Moda* is the satisfaction experienced when a desired object is obtained or attained. *Pramoda* is the memory of that satisfaction.

If *Annamaya* is equated with or regarded as the gross body, *Prana*, *Mano* and *Vijnana Kosa*s together form the subtle body or *linga Sarira*. In the *Ananda Kosa* or when man is in the deep sleep, the causal body is reached.

The *Chetana* or consciousness in the subtle body of the individual is known as *Taijasa*. **The same consciousness in its all-pervasive aspect in all living souls combinedly is called *Hiranyagarbha*,** as also the *Sutratman*. One who meditates on his simultaneous existence in the three subtle *kosas* would be meditating on *Hiranyagarbha* and when he leaves this world would reach *Brahma Loka* ruled by HIM. In that realm, he has access to all the secrets of creation. He is not reborn again on earth. If, by imperfection in his *Tapas*, he cannot reach *Brahma Loka*, he reaches the *Tapoloka*, the realm immediately below *Brahma Loka*.

These five sheaths are, of course, not the pure *Atman* or *Brahman*. Since they have qualities, the *Brahma Sutra* states *Aanandamayo Abhyaasaat* (1.12), meaning *Anandamaya* from proximity, showing that this *Anandamaya* is an attachment to or close attribute of the supreme *Brahman*. In the *Taittiriya Upanishad* the same truth is stated, as *Brahmapuchcham Pratistha* meaning that *Brahman* is behind this *Anandamaya Kosa*. Meditation on the supreme *Brahman* while inside the *Anandamaya Kosa* grants the ultimate *Brahman* experience. It is only an approximation to say that it is the causal body and also *Paramatman*.

In the case of a Yogi, his entry into *Ananda Kosa* is the fourth state of consciousness (*Turiya*) and close to *Brahman*. Only when he is able both to reach the *Anandamaya Kosa* and enter inside it, he can enjoy *Asampragjnaata Samaadhi*, the highest *Samadhi* beyond all thought. If the *Ananda Kosa* does not open out for him, the Yogi's *Samadhi* still contains the ego-consciousness, *Asmita*.

4.4 *Asvamedha Yaga*: *Yaga* with Yoga concept: Retracing the Steps of Creation

Suresvara's Vartika on *Sankara's* commentary on the *Brihadaranyaka Upanishad* is relevant here. The subject is *Asvamedha Kratu* or the horse-sacrifice. The gist of it is thus:

One should know the spirit of the *Asvamedha Kratu* in addition to its physical details. *Prajapati* (figuratively) performed this ritual at the beginning of time, obviously, as a preamble to creation. He identified his own body with that of a horse. He conceived of time, space and the worlds as parts of the horse's body. He conceived the Creator *Brahma* as a co-performer of the sacrifice along with himself. He performed a secondary sacrifice by conceptually putting his own consciousness into the horse. He also, by his creative imagination, placed the various worlds into the horse that were to be later attained and filled by him. Then he let the horse free to wander for a period of one year and when the horse returned, *Prajapati* sacrificed the horse while dwelling himself in it with his mind.

It should be understood that the soul of the horse, which was already universalised by identifying it with all elements of the creation, left its limited physical body to become one with the whole creation which, in effect, is liberation from rebirth as an individual soul. Conceptually speaking, again, the horse that was killed was Prajapati of limitations or himself, who then spreads himself up into the creation, which can only occur through his own self-multiplication and pervasive power. He thus attained all the worlds by and through self-sacrifice. He then offered several other animals in the same manner identifying each organ of his body with a particular deity. *Prajapati* thus became a combination of all the Devas or spiritual entities.

For this reason, humans who offer a horse in sacrifice to *Prajapati* satisfy all the Gods. Those who perform such a sacrifice understandingly and meaningfully, conquer death forever. For this, they must realize that the real horse that is offered is their own qualified and limited self and its attachments. The *Asvamedha* has been described as a means of attaining higher worlds iike *Bhuvar Loka*, *Agni Loka* and *Vayu Loka* and beyond all these, the *Brahma Loka*. The *Jivatman* can also attain the supreme *Brahman* through it by further meditation without ritual.

A more complete explication of this cryptic ritual is as follows: The first stage of creation was the release of the 'cosmic egg' or *Brahmanda* by *Hiranyagarbha* representing the cosmic subtle body. The description of *Prajapati* performing the *Asvamedha* is symbolic of the creation being occupied by him, through his entry into every part of it so as to become its ruler and governor. The Creator entered into his own creation — *Tat sristvaa tadevaanu praavisat.* Having created he entered into it, thereby becoming the creation's *Antaryami* or in-dwelling spirit. The *Slokas* from 212 to 218 of *Suresvara's Vartika* (on the *Sankara's* commentary on *Brihadaranyaka*) are as follows:

Esh'a evam yathaatattvam asvamedham viveda yah
Vakshyamaanena roopena veda vidyaadatastathaa

Aatmaanamasvam sankalpya kaalalokaadi dharminam
Tathaavidha sarirah sansarvalokapitaamahah

Yajeya masvamedhena bhooyo apeetyabhyamanyata
Bhoorlokaadhyaatmikam so asvamaatmaanam niravagraham

Yaavadabdam mumochaasvam svachchandam muktabandhanam
Tatah samvatsaraadoordhvam tam chaapyaalabhataatmanne

Svaatmanavayavabhootaabhyo devataabhyo yathayatham
Graamyaaranyaan pasoon praadaadanyaabhyah sa prajaapatih

Yato akarodviraadevam tasmaadeveha yaagjnikaah
Prokshitam sarvadevatyam praajaapatyam turangamam

Aalabhante yatastasmaat yathaavyaakhyaata tattvavit
Kuryaadevam yathoktaartham mrityutva pratipitsayaa

At that point of time before anything had come into being there was, of course, no such animal known as a 'horse'.

'*Aatmaanam asvam sankalpya*' means that he imagined himself to be a horse with attributes like the worlds of creation to be in order to become the element of time that governs the event of creation (in Vedic thought the horse is often a symbol of time). In other words, 'the horse' was the principle of the creation itself. The creation was then endowed with the attributes i.e., the sun, the wind, the *Vaisvanara* fire, the year, *Dyuloka* (heaven), *Antariksha* (the intervening space between the earth and the higher worlds), the directions, the elements of time like the year, and the electricity or lightning - which are the necessary ingredients in a creation to house various living creatures. This creation then reached the second stage of creation with these attributes.

He, *Hiranyagarbha* himself, became *Prajapati*, when He entered into the creation by imparting the said attributes to it. This process occupied the time known as '*Samvatsara*' or the divine year. This is the third stage of creation described as *Prajapati* leaving the created horse free for one year. For the creator to pass from His primary stage (*Hiranyagarbhah samavartataagre*), to the stage of securing His own presence with the embodied souls (*Prajaapatischarati garbhe antah*), there was an element of time introduced into the creation. This 'original time' we can experience is a vehicle that we can use to take us back to origins of creation.

At the end of the year *Prajapati*, having already entered into the horse of his own creation, killed the horse. This is to say that the horse that was conceived as the ingredients of the creation was spiritually dismembered in order to release those same factors like the sun, the directions of space, time and so on. Thus, the primordial egg that contained the seed principles of a potential creation evolved into the actual creation by the intervention of the Creator himself at a second stage.

This creation then consisted of the stars, sun, planets, the space above the plane of the earth orbit around the sun (*Dyu Loka*), higher worlds meant for more evolved (divine) beings, the heaven farther above, the still higher worlds above the pole star region, and *Brahma Loka* - the region of the Creator. The element of time, the periodicity of the revolutions of the heavenly bodies and the conditions congenial for life and intelligence, came into being to facilitate the evolution of souls steeped in *Tamas* (ignorance), to enable them to evolve through the process of rebirth into the final state of total release and merger with the Creator.

By the symbolic killing of the horse of his own creation for the purpose of releasing the variegated creation, *Prajapati* assumed the role of death also. This element of death is a necessary ingredient to guarantee that souls pass through bodily incarnations in quick succession in order to evolve into their next higher stage of experiencing nature. Every human body is, thus, a step in the ladder of evolution for the soul and the so-called death is nothing but a movement to the next rung without which the souls would only stagnate. The Creator himself, therefore, is the active principle of death, which is an evolutionary principle of consciousness.

While this is the process of nature governing all souls, Vedic knowledge created a special ritual known as the '*Asvamedha*', parallel to the original process of creation to enable a man to achieve the ultimate stage of evolution in one stroke. This is one of the many paths invented by Vedic science, like Yoga, *Tapas* of various kinds, and other Vedic sacrifices. Such paths are like the invention of airplanes to avoid the tedious process of walking on the ground to reach a distant destination. The *Asvamedha* is thus a simulation of the entire process of creation in which the performer enters into the primordial '*Prajapati* horse' by conscious effort (meditation or *Dhyana*). He then releases himself from this cosmic horse after identifying himself with *Prajapati*. The various parts of the horse are offered to the respective *Devas* in the higher worlds. The soul in the horse is one with *Prajapati* and the performer accompanying it reaches the limits of creation, having released himself from the law of rebirth. Thus, when he drops his mortal body he is not reborn on the earth. This is a rational explanation of the spirit and theory of the horse-sacrifice.

It has been said in various commentaries that since *Hiranyagarbha* or *Brahma* is the goal of mergence for the sacrificer, he would only reach *Brahma Loka* but not the unqualified *Brahman*. Elsewhere, however, it has been explained that the individual soul who sets his goal as absorption into the supreme *Brahman* can achieve it by being helped by *Vayu* to cross the limits of the *Brahmanda*.

Let us note that the *Brahmanda* is a finite entity existing and functioning as a unit in the infinite space and that there are innumerable such *Brahmandas*. The infinite space and its primary cause are the supreme *Brahman* that alone could conceive these *Brahmandas*. The soul's merger in it would be a point of no return.

The performer of the *Asvamedha* seeking such dissolution must meditate on the supreme *Brahman*. He would, at the time of leaving his body, pierce through the *Brahmarandhra* situated at the centre of the crown of the head. The human body itself is created as a miniature *Brahmanda* and therefore, the gateway situated on the tip of the *Brahmanda* into the unqualified *Brahman* beyond, is contained in this *Brahmarandhra* of the human body. It is, therefore, clear that the *Asvamedha* ritual facilitates the soul to reach the ends of creation. The Yoga, at the last moment, helps one to cross the limits of creation to the supreme *Brahman*.

We should realise that Vedic ritualism, Yogic knowledge of the secrets of the physical creation, the cosmological secrets revealed in *Sankhya*, the Vedantic explanation of the *Brahman*, and the theories about God contained in the *Upanishads* are all complimentary to each other and not differing paths. They should be understood together as one total subject. This must be obvious to us because all these teachings are derived from *Veda* in its four sectional contents of *Samhita*, *Brahmana*, *Aranyaka* and *Upanishad*. It would be wrong for the pure philosopher dwelling on the secrets of the unqualified *Brahman* as a means of *Moksha* to dismiss the *Yoga-Sankhya* combination or the Yoga-ritual combination, as incorrect or unhelpful.

It is certainly true that Vedanta reflects the highest theoretical analysis of the ultimate truth, attempting to take man to the ultimate wisdom. The theory implied in it is that knowledge of the ultimate truth, through which we can reject the lesser and relative truths about this material creation, results in the attainment of the highest wisdom. There is, however, always a thin edge separating true wisdom from mere knowledge. It requires the individual's total freedom from and transcending of all material bonds that the man's existence had struck roots into. A matter of primary consideration in all paths, therefore, is the man's stage of ripening before being initiated. In order to be released from the strong grip of nature, one should become free from the *Samskaras* responsible for any kind of conditioning.

This discussion is offered to explain why there was once a time when the Vedic *Yajna* of various descriptions existed and was observed together with an inner, conscious practice with *Moksha* as the goal to be attained either as a *Krama Mukti* (gradual release) or as direct release.

The Katha Upanishad offers such a unique path of a Ritual-*Yoga* combination in which the ritual helps conquer the evil results of physical death thus granting **an uninterrupted continuity of the self-same consciousness of the** Yogi. The *Upanishad* also offers Yoga as a superior and exclusive path to *Moksha* by adherence to the *Pranava Om* in the Yogic heart-centre. With Yoga as the inner sacrifice to complement the outer or ritual sacrifice, a complete path is offered addressing all aspects of our nature and of the world nature.

4.5 The story of *Bhujyu* and the *Sukla Yajurveda*

Relating to the efficacy of the *Asvamedha*, the *Brihadaranyaka Upanishad III.3* narrates an interesting incident:

A Brahmin by name *Bhujyu*, while questioning the Rishi *Yajnavalkya*, told him the following story. "As a student in search of learning, I toured the Madra country (northwest India) and in the course of my travels, I visited the house of one Patanchala of the Kapya clan. His daughter was then possessed by a *Gandharva*, *Sudhanva* by name. As he revealed his identity when questioned, I asked him what had happened to the progeny of King Parikshit (after they had performed Aswamedha). Can you, Oh Sage Yajnavalkya! Tell me where the sons of Parikshit have reached?"

Yajnavalkya replied, "Oh Bhujya! That Gandharva has informed you that the sons of Parikshit went where performers of the *Asvamedha* go." So saying, Yajnavalkya described the higher worlds and their limits with authority and added, "Those who have this secret knowledge would, once they leave the physical body forever conquer death," thereby indicating the great benefit of the *Asvamedha*.

This incident (narrated in 3rd Brahmana in the III chapter of the *Upanishad*) indicates the divine vision of Rishi Yajnavalkya and what is more, the superior knowledge of higher beings like *Gandharvas* about the paths of the souls of men in the universe. It has been said that the sons and grandsons of King Parikshit as a result of the *Asvamedha* transcended the higher worlds that form the body of *Virat Purusha*, by piercing through the *Brahmarandhra* described as the junction point of the *Anda* (egg) of the human body in *Kapaala* (the crown of the skull). An exit through this small narrow point enables the soul to cross beyond all *Karma Lokas* (worlds ruled by the results of *karma*) and the entire *Brahmanda* to enter into the supreme *Brahman*. Of course, the *Asvamedha* was accompanied by internal Yoga practices.

A relevant question in this regard is why such an inquiry was made to the *Gandharva* by Bhujya regarding the state of Parikshit's sons and grandsons. And why was the question referred to Yajnavalkya without first revealing the *Gandharva's* reply, as if to test his divine vision. We discover from the *Matsya Purana* (Chapter-51) that there was, in those days, a controversy among the Brahmins related to the newly acquired *Sukla Yajurveda*. Yajnavalkya acquired this *Veda* directly from the Sun God and propagated it; because he had to abandon the *Krishna Yajurveda* taught him by *Vaysampayana*, as a result of a dispute with him.

Parikshit, Janamejaya and his sons, although devoted to *Vysampayana* earlier, invited and appointed a '*Sukla Yajurveda Brahmin*' (*Vajasaneyi*) as the chief priest in the *Asvamedha* performed by them. *Vysampayana*, angered by this, cursed Janamejaya to be unauthorised to perform the *Asvamedha* and his priest to be unqualified. Janamejaya, then, performed a *Purnamasa* or full moon ritual to propitiate *Prajapati* and earned his grace. Then, Janamejaya and his son Satanika performed the *Asvamedha* in accordance with the *Sukla Yajurveda*. This led to the division among the Brahmins, many of whom joined to serve the king. *Janamejaya* earned fame as '*Mahavajasaneya*' by his supporting this tradition of the *Sukla Yajur Veda*. Perhaps, however, a doubt lingered in the minds of some *Brahmins* as to whether *Asvamedha* performed in the new *Vajasaneya*-manner would be efficacious. Hence, the question was put to a superior being, a *Gandharva*, for verification. It was certified again by Yajnavalkya, the author of the new path, himself.

The crossing of the borders of the *Brahmanda* is achieved with the help of *Vayu*, because air is the only element that can transcend the limits of the *Brahmanda*. Significantly, Yogic science tells us that the *Anaahata Chakra* is covered by the element of *Vayu* or air symbolised by the *Bijakshara* '*Yam*'.

The principle governing death is the Almighty Himself. In the *Brihadaranyaka Upanishad*, the words *Asva* (horse), *Arka* (ray of light), *Samudra* (ocean), *Aditi* (boundless space) and *Mrityu* (death) are all synonymous with *Prajapati* who is none other than *Hiranyagarbha*, the Creator and Sustainer and the Killer or Destroyer. This again is the *Paramatman*, the supreme Self, who is the *Antaratman* or inner Self within us.

These various names are functional aspects of one power. A further elaboration follows for the benefit of readers quoting from *Suresvara's Vartika* on *Sankara's* commentary on '*Asvamedha Brahmana*':

Upaasanasya svaatantryat karmanaadhikritopi cha
Manasaa kalpayitvaasvam viraadrupena chintayet
(Brihadaranyaka Vartikasara by Vidyaranya: V-18)

Kartaara masvamagnim cha chityam sarva prajaapatim
Asvamedha phalamchaarkam vetti mrityum yathoditam
(Suresvara's Vartika on Asvamedha Brahmana: 1.1.5)

Akartaapyasvamedhasya braahmanascheha buddhimaan
Kratvaatmaa mrityurasmeeti taadaatmyam so adhigachchati
(Suresvara's Vartika on Asvamedha Brahmana: 1.1.6)

And the wise *Brahmin*, even though a non-performer of the *Asvamedha*, who knows about the spirit of the sacrifice, to him the horse and the fire are *Prajapati*, *Arka* and the result of the *Asvamedha* is *Mrityu* (the God of Death). It secures oneness with Him (*Mrityu* or the *Sutratman*) on knowing 'I am the soul of the sacrifice, *Mrityu*'.

Thus, with or without the external ritual, the *Antaryaaga* or inner ritual is of primary importance for the achievement of the object. This secret principle in the ritual is of great and paramount importance.

5. NACHIKETA'S YOGA

5.1 Yoga and *Om*

The human body is miniature universe (*Kshudra Brahmanda*) hence containing the higher worlds in spirit. In the *Yoga Sastra* path, the Yogi conquers and crosses the *Bhuloka* at the *Muladhara chakra*, *Agni Loka* at the *Svadhisthana*, *Vayu Loka* at the *Manipura* and reaching *Dahara Akasa*, the small space within the heart, by crossing all the regions of the earlier *Lokas* lying on its border in a subtle form, he enters that space within and by the appropriate *Sadhana* there — the practice of *Pranava* (*Om*) — attains *Brahman* itself. The efficacy of *Pranava* is repeatedly stressed in the entire Yoga literature and also in the *Puranas*. But in this *Upanishad* the immediate benefit gained by *Upasana* of *Pranava* after conquering the pain of death is the main thing. That is why *Pranava* is described in the later portions, fourth, fifth and sixth *Vallis* of this Katha Upanishad as "*Om iti etat*" repeatedly. In this connection it is relevant to quote from '*Siva jnanamrita Upanishad*'. The ninth *mantra* is as follows:

Saanubhavam saarthaanusandhaanam cha pranavamaatroyam
Adhyaatma maarge tarati sarvaanantaraayaan
Hrasvah pranavah sarva paapaapanodanah
Deergho muktipradah pluto akhila siddhihetuh

Repetition of *Om* with meaning and *Bhava* will remove all obstacles in the path. Short intonation destroys all sins, long intonation containing two or three *matras* leads to knowledge. *Pluta* — an elongated intonation of three *matras* — grants all *Siddhis* and liberation too.

While this is purely a Yogic path, Vedic sacrifices accompanied by such inner practices, along with an understanding of the spiritual significance of the practice, are bound to result in the permanent attainment of the higher *Lokas* and also final emancipation. This concept applies to the *Nachiketa Agni* ritual, which means that when a performer of it leaves his body, he identifies himself with death itself and therefore does not die. Instead, releasing himself voluntarily from his physical body, he becomes deathless forever. By virtue of his earlier *Sadhana* and transcending the subtle *Loka*-centres within, he reaches and crosses beyond the higher worlds, and through the appropriate *Sadhana* of *Om* attains the supreme *Brahman*.

In the other case, when the performer of the Nachiketa-sacrifice, after transcending the subtle worlds within, through Yoga and reaching the heart-centre by crossing the peripheral rings of air and fire around it, he enters into the *Dahara Akasa* through the practice of *Om* to be finally absorbed into the *Brahman* of the inner space. This is achieved during his physical existence here on earth.

While in the body, the *Jivatman* exists on the strength of the life force, which is limited in its sphere of activity. Since the same life force pervades all space in creation, the *Jivatman* that leaves the body must sustain itself as an individual on the all-pervading life force. Whether it is inside or outside of the body, the *Atman* needs life-energy in order to exist as an individual *Jiva*. In the absence of the life force, the soul or *Atman* cannot be a *Jivatman*. **The word '*Jeevati*' indicates '*living*'. *Jivatman* lives, while *Atman* only exists**.

One who has conquered death by identifying himself with death at the time of leaving the body, moves in the worlds with knowledge of the mystery of all creation as a *Jivatman* without a body. He is a conscious soul without a body and gifted with knowledge. Such *Jiva* fits the description — *Jivo Brahmaiva naa parah*. This *Upanishad* in its later portions repeatedly stresses the importance of *Pranava* (Om) as a means of liberation.

5.2 Nachiketa Agni and Yoga

Trinaachiketah tribhiretya sandhim
Trikarmakruttarati janmamrityoo
Brahmajagjnam devameedyam viditvaa
Nichaayya maagm saantimatyantameti
(Katha Upanishad: 1.17)

The *Yoga Sastra* of *Patanjali* is positive in its message that God (*Isvara*) can be realized by *Upasana* (meditative worship) of *Om*. The Katha Upanishad as traditionally being a '*Yoga Upanishad*' stresses the power of *Om* as the giver of liberation. Before providing final directions about liberation through *Om*, the Lord of Death teaches the threefold *Nachiketa Agni*, the fire ritual, and the piercing of the three knots — *Brahma*, *Vishnu* and *Rudra granthis* — in the *Chakras* or plexuses inside the body. This *Yoga*-ritual combination serves as a preamble to *Moksha Sadhana*.

Although Nachiketa said that he has no material desires and is only interested in knowing the secrets of death, it is interesting to note that he **did** ask for a return to his father, his father's affection to him, life in *Svarga* where there is no death (Yama's presence) and also *Istaapoorta* (the fulfillment of all desires normally obtained by pleasing the Gods). These desires had to be granted before he became eligible for *Moksha*. For these to be gained *Nachiketa Agni* is indicated. With these he is simply expressing his *samskaras* as the deeper desires of the soul.

5.3 The *Agni* Ritual, its Details and Meaning

The *Taittiriya Brahmana* (*Astaka*-3, *Prapaathaka*-11) deals with the *Nachiketa Chayana*. This has three stages. The first stage (*Anuvaaka*-8) grants all the material happiness possible in human life. It involves the arrangement of the bricks with *Mantras* starting with the words *Lokosi*, meaning 'you are the world'. It grants men happiness equal to that of the gods. In the second stage, the arrangement of the bricks is done with the *Mantras* — *Aaposi* and *Tejosi* meaning 'you are water' and 'you are fire'. This part of the ritual grants the performer the entry into *Dyu Loka* (the realm of heaven). This is an achievement primarily to avoid going to *Pitruloka* (the manes), which necessitates a return to *Bhuloka* (earth), even if he is destined to reach the higher worlds in the northern half of *Brahmanda.*

Dyu Loka is the threshold to the heavens of the *Devas*, who worship the *Brahma Deva* directly. Hence, these regions are known as *Hiranyarupa* or golden in form. Mortal men on earth worship the same *Devas* for lesser benefits and the fulfillment of ordinary desires.

In the third stage, eighteen bricks are arranged with the *mantras* — *Samudrosi*, meaning 'you are the ocean'. This enables the performer to reach the sphere of the Sun (*Aditya Mandala)* from which he can access the higher worlds beyond death. This, in brief, is the *Trinaachiketaagni.* It fulfils all the desires that Nachiketa sought from the Lord of Death.

5.4 Crossing the Three Junctures (Tribhiretya Sandhim)

In normal Yoga practice the three junction points of *Brahma*, *Vishnu* and *Rudra* are pierced after entering into the *Sushumna nadi.*

Muladhara and *Svadhisthana* control the earthy and the fiery elements respectively but together are known as the *Agni Khanda*, the region of fire. They are knotted together at *Brahma granthi* or knot of Brahma.

Manipura and *Anaahata* centres are the watery and airy elements respectively, comprising the region of *Surya Khanda*, the realm of the Sun, and are knotted together at *Vishnu granthi* or knot of Vishnu.

Visuddha and *Aajna* centres are the sky and the mind elements respectively, comprising the region known as

Chandra Khanda, the realm of the Moon, and are knotted together at *Rudra granthi* or the knot of Rudra-Siva.

These three knots must be crossed sequentially in order to become independent of the three *Gunas* of *Tamas*, *Rajas* and *Sattva*. The goal of crossing them is to attain equanimity or balancing the three *Gunas*, which causes the Soul's interaction with *Prakriti* to cease. The unequal state of the *Gunas*, with their interaction and combination in an unlimited variety, results in the soul's experience of nature, whether in earthly existence or in higher worlds of so-called happiness (which are also not permanent).

Another achievement gained by balancing the *Gunas* is that the *Jivatman* goes beyond the limitations of the gross and subtle bodies and reaches the causal body (*Kaarana Sarira*), where the unqualified *Brahman* can be meditated upon using *Om* as both the path and the goal. If the three *Gunas* reach a perfect equilibrium in a man, no experiential state in the creation can arise within him. In the case of the cosmic creation, the cause of all material experience is the inequality in these *Gunas*. The dissolution of the creation follows from their perfect equalisation.

In the case of the Yogi, the equilibrium of the three *Gunas* can take him to the state of unqualified/unconditioned being; but he is yet to achieve the ultimate dissolution in *Brahman* (which requires taking refuge in *Om*), so that he would not come back into the phenomenal existence. This Yoga, therefore, consists of two stages — one, conquering the rebirth phenomenon, and two, attaining *Moksha*. The second one is an achievement, according to the Lord of Death, to be realised in the *Anaahata* or Heart centre.

From the foregoing discussion it is clear conquering the six centres and piercing the three knots, is not the final achievement. In the case of the performer of *Asvamedha* also, concentration and meditation on the supreme *Brahman* while leaving the body through the *Brahmarandhra* is the way to dissolution in *Brahman*, because he crosses the limits of the *Brahmanda*.

5.5 *Anaahata*

In the message of the Katha Upanishad, the Lord of Death is pointing to the secret of the *Anaahata*, accompanied by the *Pranava Om* as the gateway to final dissolution. *Anaahata*, therefore, is the prime subject matter of this *Upanishad*.

The *Yoga Sastra* describes this *Anaahata* as a twelve petalled lotus. The instruction, for the convenience of the Yogi, is that he should imagine such a lotus with twelve petals in the heart-centre and circumambulate it with his mind, dwelling one by one on the sounds of its different letters from *kam* to *tham*. This dwelling on each sound of the petals in repeated conscious circumambulations must be done adequately to obtain oneness of the mind with the sounds. Dwelling on such sounds means with full attention inwardly, not that one should physically utter them. It means that one should try to hear them from within in a state of silence. This is done, of course, with controlled breath. Such is the mental utterance.

The *Sadhana* of *Anaahata Chakra* is an established Yogic practice, known to Yogis and need not be elaborated here. The relevant point is that the first and last letters of its twelve petals existing side by side in the circular arrangement give us the name *KA-THA*. Thus, the name of *Anaahata* itself is *Katha*. Since the very subject matter of the *Upanishad* is *Anaahata*, we can even infer that the *Upanishad* is named as *KATHA*, after the two *Bijaksharas* of the heart *chakra*.

5.6 Reaching Higher Worlds through Yoga

The Yogi, who intends to travel in space and reach the higher worlds, must enter into that element, which pervades and extends to the higher worlds starting from the earth. Such element that reaches up to *Svarga* or heaven is *Agni* or fire, while element of air reaches up to and beyond *Brahma Loka*, and the element of *Akasa* or ether reaches to the ends of the *Brahmanda*. In the process of reaching the *Svadhisthana*, for example, the Yogi has entered into the element and medium of the 'fire' principle. Similar is the path to the higher worlds.

6. THE SELF WITHIN THE HEART AND THE PATHS OF YOGA

6.1 *Sankhya* and Yoga

Sankhya philosophy, (which classical Yoga also shares) asserts a duality between God and the soul and that the souls are manifold. Nature or *Prakriti* is enjoyed by the soul or *Purusha* as the enjoyer (*Bhokta)*. In *Vaishnavism* in which God is worshipped in the form of *Vishnu*, the *Jivatman* who concentrates his devotion on *Vishnu* attains *Vishnu Loka*, gaining proximity to *Vishnu*. Thus, losing his *Jivatmic*-state, he assumes the form of *Vishnu* himself, forever remaining in a dualistic state, but enjoying the bliss of *Vishnu*-hood or similitude with *Vishnu* or the Supreme God. In *Saivism*, the theory is similar except that the devotee of *Siva* gets absorbed in *Siva*.

In fact, *Upasana* (internal worship) of a deity like *Vishnu*, *Siva* or *Sakti* in any form will remove the personal ego-consciousness of the *Jivatman* and grant it the form-consciousness of its object of devotion. In all these paths, the worship, devotion and constant 'self-surrender' to the respective God-form, together with the chanting of the appropriate mantra are prescribed. The nature of soul is such:

Nainam chindanti sastraani nainam dahati paavakah
Na chainam kledayantyaapo na soshayati maarutah

(Gita, II.23)

The soul is not harmed by weapons or burned by fire, nor is made wet by water or dried up by the wind.

It is surrounded by an aura — a nebulous field of its *Samskaras* made up of its memories and tendencies. This is ephemeral and is different from the soul.

In the physical body, the region of the souls' movement is from *Muladhara* to the heart-centre, but staying nowhere steady even for a moment. His location is governed by the various states of consciousness like sleep, dream and waking and the activities during these states. This *Angustha Purusha* is the *Jivatman* in his outer shape and *Paramatman* at the core, simultaneously. It is for this reason that *Angustha Purusha* is also described as God himself. He is at once deathless in his essence but dying in his body — association.

The Atman at the core of the subtle body is basis for the experiences of the 'inch-man', Angustha Purusha or Jivatman. The Upanishad's description that there are two birds — one experiencing the body and the other remaining detached as its silent witness — is allegorical and refers to the condition when the Jivatman is dwelling in the body. Thus, the state of duality is always ephemeral, interrupted by death but lasting up to the point of liberation. A state that can be interrupted for a while and revived again is obviously false.

Naasato vidyate abhaavo naabhaavo vidyate satah
Ubhayorapi dristho anthastvanayoh tattvadarsibhih

(Gita, II.16)

There can be no non-being of that which truly exists. There can be no true existence of that which can be absent at a time.

The *Angustha Purusha* is also the *sukshma Sarira* or subtle body. He is the doer and enjoyer by his interaction with the outer world through the medium of the physical senses. The *Sankalpa*, desire tendency or disposition of a person, makes a man anything from a sage to a criminal. What he loses at the time of death is his external form and later, the replica of his physical body also, but the core point in him that has no shape carries these tendencies as the essence of the bygone life on the earth. He carries the seed of the future tree. Let us remember again, however, that this core point is nothing but an essential reflection of the *Paramatman*, the all-pervading only Truth of the creation.

Apart from the Jivatman that is not fixed but in constant movement in the region from Muladhara to the heart region, there is an empty space inside the heart-lotus, within the Sushumna-path. This Dahara Akasa (small space) or Sunya-sthana (region of the void) is the void or space at the centre of the heart, inside the lotus formation within the Sushumna Nadi. Its physical dimensions as sized-up from the outside are infinitesimal, but when the Yogi consciously enters it, it is a vast world in itself. This Akasa is pervaded by a Nada or 'universal hum', which is defined as Om. And hence, one who meditates on this sound can enter into this space and become universal.

This small space contains the subtle or causal forms, as the Yogic Science asserts, of the elements of wind, fire, and so on, governed by the respective deities, Isana and Kakini. The operative lever to these elements is the Bijaakshara. For example, the terrific current of wind surrounding the periphery of the Heart Chakra, making entry inside impossible for a Yogi's consciousness, is calmed down by the Bijaakshara 'Yam'. Before this, however, he has to meditate on the individual petals of the lotus. (In the ordinary state of the human being, the lotus of the Heart faces downwards as a hanging bud and only when awakened, does it turn upwards to unfold itself.) This affords the Yogi a greater preparedness and ability to enter into the lotus. Every letter on the petals, when meditated upon gives him greater ability to pierce through it.

6.2 The Path of Devotion to the Form of God

In this process, the subtle body or *sukshma sarira* or *Angustha Purusha* or *Jivatman* is traveling inward to the original *Paramatman* referred to as *Antaryami* — the indweller. Even before a conscious union is achieved, a vision of the original *Paramatman* inside can destroy the karma of the *Jivatman* forever. If this core truth is imagined as a God-form like *Vishnu or Rudra* and meditated upon with devotion, the man experiences visions of these deities and also of the Lokas associated with them. This is described as *Saalokya* (sharing the same world with forms of *Paramatman*).

According to this path, without such an experience, the *Jivatman* has no other way of destroying its Karma. The compulsions of nature to go through the results of one's karma do not affect the *Jivatman* in the achieved presence of the qualified or unqualified *Paramatman* inside the realm of the heart-centre. The karmic law does not work there. The *Paramatman* is, therefore, the causal body common in all living creatures. It is often described in the literature that the *Paramatman* is the same whether it is in the body of an ant or Lord *Brahma*. Even for the *Jivatman*, there is no such thing as real death or birth, only transmigration. The core being itself continues.

When the *Samskaras* or memories of the world are totally destroyed, the cause of rebirth is forever removed. The law of rebirth of a soul is governed by the presence of *Paramatman* in himself as witness to the actions of the *Jivatman*. If nature with its five elements is comparable to the ocean, a living body, whether of a human or an animal, is like a wave. The contents of the wave and the ocean are the same, and yet the wave is not the ocean. No wave, which is transitory in its existence, is repeated while the ocean is permanent. Similarly, in the physical sense, no human being returns. All these fundamental truths must be remembered before one is able to comprehend this *Upanishad*.

6.3 Brahma Sutras: The *Jivatman*

The interrelationship and oneness of the *Jivatman* and *Paramatman*, is the main subject of the *Brahma Sutras*. Under the subchapter *Pramitaadhikaranam* (1.3) the *Angustha Purusha* has been directly dealt with. *Pramita* means the measurability of the dimensions or attributes of the *Jivatman*. How can the unlimited *Paramatman* assume a thumb-sized form inside the human body? Is this *Angustha Purusha* – *Jivatman* — different from *Paramatman*? Katha Upanishad (4.12) says —

Angusthamaatrah purusho madhya aatmani tisthati
Esaano bhootabhavyasya na tato vijugupsate
Etat vai tat

The Purusha of the size of a thumb dwells at the core of oneself. He is the Lord of his past and future. Knowing him one is no more disturbed by anything.

The *Angustha Purusha* situated in the centre of one's being is the master of the past and the future. This means that the past births and future existence of the *Jivatman* are accompanied and governed by Him alone. He is *Isvara*, the omnipotent and omnipresent by being present inside every *Jiva*; hence the word *Jivatman* — the soul's god. In essence, it points to *Brahman* as well. Like the space in a pot, it is possible for the *Paramatman* to assume an apparent measurable size. This 'size' is the specialised attribute of the *Paramatman*. This apparent condition of the *Paramatman* is the natural quality of the *Jivatman*. It should be understood that the *Jivatman* has a conditioned and limited size in the body. And the *Paramatman* is also present as a bright point of no dimensions, situated inside the *Jivatman*.

The changes of state like waking, sleep and dream, as well as the postures that go with a measurable size, are natural attributes of *Jivatman*, while no such changes are attributable to the *Paramatman* being only a point in the centre of *Jivatman*. Body consciousness, therefore, is of the *Jivatman* alone. He is the indweller of the five concentric sheaths or *Kosas*, namely, *Annamaya*, *Pranamaya*, *Manomaya*, *Vijnanamaya* and *Anandamaya*. Even in his state of presence in the *Anandamaya Kosa*, the *Paramatman* remains only a dot.

Even when the *Jivatman* transmigrates from one body to another it carries this *Paramatman* within itself. It is He who is the witness to the soul's *Karma*, its results, its position in various *Lokas*, its activity and its process of living etc. This witness is also the governing force that yields the results of karma to the *Jivatman*. This is to say that the *Jivatman* is not independent and free, but is governed by *Paramatman* with whom it is inseparable in essence obviously he is not different from HIM. The commentary in the *Brahma Sutras* concludes that, this *Jivatman* is *Paramatman* himself. *Sri Ramanuja* asserts that he is *Vishnu* himself. But then the question arises how Lord Yama, the God of Death, is capable of pulling this *Jivatman* (if he is the Almighty God himself) out with his noose as evidenced by the case of *Savitri's* husband and others?

Sri Sankaracharya's assertion that this *Angustha Purusha* is *Isvara* does not mean that there is nothing like a *Jivatman*. It means that the two exist inseparably being aspects of one and the same truth. Moreover, Vedanta explains that *Isvara* is *Maya's* reflection in the pure *Brahman* and the *Jiva* is *Isvara's* reflection in the five-element based *Prakriti*. But if *Jivatmans* are nothing but a reflection of *Isvara*, for whose benefit is the Creation? In *Brahma Sutras* (1.2) *Attradhikaranam*, the *Sutra* says '*Guhaam pravishtau aatmaanau hi taddarsanaat*'. Using the dual case, it states that the *Jiva* and *Paramatman* together have entered the heart-cave.

One more quotation from the *Brahma Sutras* is relevant in this regard — '*Aatmaa antaraatmeti harireka eva dvidhaa sthitah nivisto hrudaye nityam sampibati karmajam'*. The meaning is that the one *Hari* (God or *Vishnu*) is in a dual state in the heart. *Atman* is *Jivatman*, which can assume a physical body and a resultant subtle body. *Antaratman* is the *Bindu* or dot inside it. '*Taddarsanaat*', in the *Sutra* is to mean that the *Jiva* should realise its inner being in order to attain true knowledge. *Kena Upanishad* describes HIM as the source of the *Jiva's* ability to see, hear, think and so forth.

In the third *Pada* of the *Sutras*, in *Daharaadhikaranam* also, the words, '*Antaraatmaa sadaa janaanaam hridaye sannivista*' (the inner Self is ever placed in the hearts of men), are examined to find whether they refer to the *Jivatman* or *Paramatman*. *Svetashvatara Upanishad* says, '*Praanaadhipah sancharati svakarmabhih Angusthamaatro ravitulya tejah sankalpaahankaara samanvitoyah*' — The inner self is ever placed in the hearts of men. *Sankalpa* and ego are the attributes of the one who lives by *Prana*. The one who is bound by karma is the *Angustha Purusha* or *Jivatman* and the *Bindu* inside which is *Aprameya* - the immeasurable — is the *Paramatman*. It is effulgent like the Sun.

Another *Sutra* says, '*Sabdaadeva pramitah*', indicating He is attributed with dimensions only in words but not virtually so in reality. But He governs the entire activity. So the thumb-size existence is the action of *Paramatman* but it is not Himself. All actions and forms are only fleeting.

The Yogi can see the *Angustha Purusha* as the reflection of his own physical body with all its functions, as a seer. Concentration of mind and consciousness on the forms of gods like *Ganapati* or *Subrahmanya* makes the *Jivatman* assume those forms, replacing the human-body identification, which is lost forever if the *Upasana* of these deities has attained or reached perfection. There can be no rebirth as a human but in the end when all the worlds and those forms are also dissolved, the *Jivatman* may be dissolved into the *Brahman* when those forms are also withdrawn. If *Brahman* is not the goal of the *Tapas* and if such qualified forms of God return into the creation, the *Jiva* may perhaps, be reborn as the *Sankhya Purusha* of the seventeen (or eighteen) attributes. But if the *Jivatman* aims at oneness with the supreme *Brahman*, the path of *Pranava* shown in this *Upanishad* can certainly help him. However, the concentration on pure *Brahman* is not as easy as the approach to qualified forms of God.

The *Sruti* says, '*Aatmaavaare drastavyah srotavyo mantavyo nidhidhyaasitavyah*' — 'the Self alone is to be seen, heard, thought about and meditated on'. This path to *Jnana* is the *Upasana* of the seeker who may, one day, succeed in experiencing the unqualified *Brahman*. But in the process, in addition to the intellectual pursuit and analysis of the truth (like the *Vedantin*), Yoga path must also be followed leading to the *Asampragjnaata samaadhi*. The Rishis of yore through *Tapas* attained the higher worlds as well as the supreme *Brahman*. They also performed *Tapas* directed to Gods like *Vishnu* and *Siva* and performed *Karma* to benefit the society. It is clear that the *srotavya, dhyatavya* and *mantavya* (what is to be heard, thought about and meditated on) is inside the *Angustha Purusha* himself, which can ultimately destroy all individualistic and separatist conditionings.

Being inseparable from the human soul, all the actions of *Jivatman* like sleep and waking, standing and running are attributable to *Paramatman* as well, he being the 'inner governing principle'. Similarly, all the states of the *Jiva*, even up to death and rebirth, are witnessed and governed by the *Paramatman*.

The *Taittiriya Aranyaka* (10.13) states:

Neevaarasookavattanvee peetabhaasvatyanoopama
Tasyaah sikhaayaa madhye Paramaatmaa vyavasthitah
Sa brahma sa siva sa hari ssendra ssoksharah paramassvaraat

Of the size of an atom, as small as the tip of a grain of rice, golden in color, extremely subtle, in the middle of the crest of that flame, the *Paramatman* dwells. He is *Brahma*, *Siva*, *Hari*, *Indra*, the *Akshara* and the supreme ruler, all at once.

The atomic sized *Paramatman* inside the heart-centre is the *Brahma*, *Siva*, *Hari*, *Indra* and all the Gods at once are described in this. These *Taittiriya mantras*, contained in 12th and 13th *Anuvaaka* (also known as the *Narayana Sukta*), provide a physical and physiological description of the location and nature of the *Paramatman* inside the heart region. *Sayanacharya*, in the tradition of *Advaita Vedanta*, states that this description is a guidance and an aid to meditation, meant for less competent aspirants who cannot achieve an understanding of the *Vedantic* analysis of the formless *Atman*. Nevertheless, the description is very much there in this *Upanishad*. This description of the heart-centre, supported by a number of statements from the *Sruti,* is only to be meditated upon, along with all the necessary austerities, and that itself leads to an experience of the supreme truth, as claimed by *Yoga Sastra*.

Briefly, these *Mantras* of the *Narayana Sukta* indicate an *Akasa* (space), inside which exists the heart-lotus (the twelve-petalled lotus of the Yogi) as the object of meditation (*Upasitavyam*). This lotus, situated below the chest region, is inverted facing downward. Its fiery brilliance pervades an extent of ten inches (an inch is thumb's top phalange length) above the navel with the heart-lotus on top. This lotus, hanging down as it were, has many fine arteries or lines of life force all sides of it. There is a super fine opening into the lotus. This is obviously the *Sushumna Nadi* touching the heart-lotus from below.

At this orifice a great fire (*Mahan Agni, Viswarchi*) exists as a bright dot, which is the sustaining fire of the man and at the same time universal. This fire tip is like an atom in size, and bright like lightning. At its top is a dot, that is the supreme God known as *Hari*, *Brahma*, *Siva* or *Indra*. This teaching is a direction for the Yogi to enter into the space inside the heart through ascent into *Sushumna*. On reaching this point the *Jivatman* with the dot of *Paramatman* in itself can unite with the unqualified *Brahman* of the said inner space. Thus, the Yoga-path to liberation, more clearly than anything else, is indicated by *Sruti*.

6.4 Prana and Sakti

The *Pranas* are the strings of life that bind the *Jivatman* to the body. They enable the *Jivatman* to handle, operate and manoeuver the body at will by taking the command from *Jivatman* through the medium of his consciousness. He operates in the body like the driver in a vehicle.

Aatmaanagm rathinam viddhi sariragm rathameva tu
Buddhim tu saarathim viddhi manah pragrahameva cha
(Katha Upanishad: 3.3)

Know that *Atman*, the Self, as the rider and body as the chariot he rides. Know the discretion (*Buddhi*) as the driver of the chariot and the mind (*Manas*) as the controlling reins.

This functional operation of the body is at its height of efficiency by virtue of the *Jivatman* totally identifying himself with it — the state of 'body consciousness' (*Dehaatma bhaavana*). This 'body consciousness' is the property of the ego, from which the stored *Samskaras* function. The operational efficiency and body-consciousness are two different aspects of the same *Chaitanya* or conscious energy. This energy again is called *Sakti* and pervades the whole creation, in which aspect it is an object of worship as the Supreme Mother. This Supreme Mother is described variously in the vast *Sakta-Yoga* literature and is an independent subject by itself.

Sakti is universal and individual at the same time. This life-energy is responsible for hunger, appetite, digestion, assimilation and conversion of matter into energy and even the intellect. The same energy is the fire-energy when it functions as the digestive power. Thus, life and energy are not different while as energy it is described in the *Sakta* cult as — '*Yaa devi sarva bhooteshu kshudhaa / nidraa / buddhi roopena samsthitaa*' (*Durga Saptasati*) — 'The Goddess who dwells in all beings as hunger, sleep, intellect and so on'. These functions of the *Jivatman* are made possible by the 'fire' element described as the Supreme Mother, which exists in all living creatures.

The same fire-energy is described as the energy of God in his own words:

Aham vaisvaanaro bhootvaa praaninaam dehamaasritah
Pranaapaana samaayuktah pachaamyannam chaturvidham

(Gita, XV.14)

Having become the *Vaisvanara* fire, I dwell in the body of all living beings.

United with *Prana* and *Apana*, I digest food in four ways.

Thus, again, the energy of the Supreme Lord runs the universal show. The Lord and his energy are inseparable like the Sun and its light, like the 'word' and its 'meaning' (*Kalidasa*). In the human body this energy or *Prana* has divided itself into four functions - A*pana*, *Udana*, *Samana* and *Vyana*. This is a functional necessity for the complex processes of life.

The *Gita* statement in this connection should be rightly understood. The commentators have often referred to the four kinds of food while commenting on the word, C*haturvidham*. It should be read as, *Pachaami Chaturvidham*. — Myself having become (*bhootvaa*) *Vaisvaanaraagni*, I assimilate the food to give rise to four different functional aspects of life; as *Udana* at the throat-centre performing the function of respiration, as *Apana* - the excretory function, as *Samana* at the navel-centre discharging the digestive and assimilative responsibilities, and as all-pervasive *Vyana Prana* causing the experience of sensations both physical and emotional.

This combination of the *Paramatman* and his energy rules the combination of individual and his body. The commanding centre of life is located at the heart-centre, known as *Mukhya* (the chief) *Prana*, where no bodily functions are discharged. At the time of death, this life-energy of the four kinds described is withdrawn into the throat-centre and then to the heart-centre where they combinedly merge into the *Mukhya-Prana*. Then the process of death is completed. Since the *Jivatman*, the soul at its center, can no longer function in the body after the withdrawal of the *Pranas*, the individual must therefore leave the body. Perforce he leaves the body.

The state of *Jivatman* between two births:

He, however, retains the body consciousness for a while by continuing in the state of *Jivatman* (*Angustha Purusha*), until that form eventually dissolves as well. This brief state is known as *Pretatva* (*Para-aetatva*). A shapeless aura remains with the core retaining all the *Karma Vasanas* in it till the *Jivatman* assumes another body and another *Angustha rupa.* This is a continually changing process of reincarnation. When the knowledge of truth is attained, this *Jivatman* assumes no more bodies. The Yogi who functions in the body as *Angustha Purusha* for purposes of normal human bodily living, but he does not identify himself with the body and is aware of his unbound *Atman.* He has no reincarnation after the body departs.

That state of *Pretatva* is administered and governed by the aspect of God known as Yama, the God of Death. In other words, the further state to be reached by the *Jivatman* without the body, in accordance with its good and bad karma, is judged, governed and executed by the God of Death who is none else than a part or aspect of the Supreme God. This principle, therefore, is known as *Paretaraat*, the king of *Pretas*. He alone, therefore is the knowledgeable *Guru* on this subject.

We have earlier said that according to the *Vedanta Sastra*, this *Jivatman* is none other than the *Paramatman* himself in his bodily function. For this reason, the *Jivatman's* states can be ascribed to the *Paramatman*. Hence it is —

Namah svapadbhyo jaagradbhyaschavo
Namah tisthadbhyo dhaavadbhyaschavo
Namah aaseenebhyah sayaanebhyascha vo namah

(Rudra Adhyaya)

Salutations to Him who sleeps, who wakes, who stands, who runs, who sits and who lies down.

The *Jivatman* or *Angustha Purusha* assumes all the postures the body takes. However, this property of the *Paramatman* is simultaneous in the bodies of all creatures. It is the universal God or *Prajapati* comprised of all creatures put together as one entity. In this context, the numerous *Jivatmans* are compared to the Sun's reflections in various pots of water. It is on this basis that we can declare that there is only one *Atman* in any body, which, in fact is the *Paramatman*.

This *Paramatman* is the core principle of even the Gods. He alone is described as *Brahma*, *Vishnu* and other Gods. That is why while praising the *Bindu* (point) with lustre within the Heart, the *Sruti* says — '*sa Brahma, sa Sivah, sa Harih, sa Indrah, sa Aksharah, Paramassvaraat*', 'He is *Brahma*, *Siva*, *Hari*, *Indra*, the *Akshara* and the supreme ruler'. This is a famous line from the *Narayana Sukta* chanted at every *Puja* to the Gods. This is the essence of the philosophy in the various texts describing God in man.

7. THE YOGA CHAKRAS AND KUNDALINI

7.1 Yoga Chakras and the Human Body

We will repeat the same description in the language of Yoga. In the physical body, the spinal or vertebral column consists of thirty-three bones of varying sizes called vertebrae. The brain is connected to this column through the medulla oblongata, the centre of which is closely connected to the involuntary respiration centres governing breath, swallowing and so on. The spinal column has seven vertebrae in cervical region (neck), twelve in the dorsal (back) region, five in the lumbar (waist) region, five in the sacral (buttocks) region and four in the coccygeal. These are connected by fibrous cartilage tissue passing through the vertebrae.

The spinal cord links the brain with a place near the second vertebrae of the coccygeal region. The *Nadi* merges into the region ending up in a coiled state around a *Linga* shape called 'filum terminale'. Before this termination it issues forth a bunch of nerves the centre of which is called *Mulakanda* or (root section) in Yoga language. At this *Kanda* there are two *Nadis* joining the *Sushumna* and they originate in the testes, near the reproductive organ. In their ascending path, these three meet closely at *Anaahata Chakra* and again at *Ajna Chakra*. Inside the spinal cord a canal passes which is called *Canalis Centralis* in anatomy and the cord itself is the hollow of the spinal column. *Sushumna* is the subtle channel of life energy passing as a current in this cord.

At the top, the central canal of the spinal cord opens into the fourth ventricle of the brain in the Medulla, runs through the third and lateral ventricles and then reaches the crown of the head, which is the *Sahasrara*. Inside the *Sushumna*, the *Vajra Nadi* passes, inside which *Chitrini Nadi* passes. Roughly this system as a whole is referred as the *Sushumna*.

The human body is a web-like work woven round the cerebro-spinal column or backbone. It starts with the centre of brain-matter and ends with the *Muladhara*, a tip below the sex organs. This bottom region is located between the sacrum and the coccyx. The lower tip of the spinal column merges into a superfine lotus whose material is not flesh, blood or bone but ethereal light. For this reason, it is not possible to x-ray its image nor is it visible to any microscope. At the centre of the lotus is a *Linga*, an extremely small thumb-like formation. The spinal column from its start from the central base of the brain and ending with the *Muladhara* carries in its core a super thin channel of light known as *Nadi*. This is the *Brahma Nadi* or the same *Sushumna Nadi*.

Starting along with the *Sushumna* in the brain-centre, two more *Nadis* known as *Ida* (the left) and *Pingala* (the right) descend, gently curved and circling around the *Brahma Nadi*, reaching the *Muladhara*. They cross each other on the *Brahma Nadi* before reaching the *Muladhara*, passing closely to it at six points, three below the Heart-centre and three above including the Heart-centre. These junction points are known as *chakras* where the three *Nadis* come close without touching or cutting each other, giving rise to a formation like a lotus made up of pure light-energy.

The *Angustha Purusha* or *Jivatman* mainly dwells close to the heart-centre but not actually within it. In day to day life, the *Jivatman* travels up and down between the *Muladhara Chakra* and the heart-centre while experiencing various states like wakefulness, sleep and dream. The body-consciousness of the *Jivatman* is due to his constant contact with the *Muladhara chakra* through the *Ida* and *Pingala Nadis*.

During the deep-sleep state the *Jivatman* often rests on the threshold of the *Sushumna Nadi* at a point very close to the

Muladhara. It may and can partly travel upward through the *Sushumna* itself in the sleep state to the *Svadhisthana* and *Manipura* regions. Due to the uninterrupted contact of the *Sushumna* with the brain-centre, the mind is thoughtless while the body is asleep. The mind's living through events of life, is called the dream-state. These mental events triggered from the *Sushumna's* contact with the brain-centre, or more precisely the *Ajna Chakra* region, may relate to the past or to the future. When no such signal is sent to the *Jivatman* in *Sushumna* from any point from the brain to *Muladhara*, the *Jivatman* dwells very close to the *Muladhara*; in which condition, the deep sleep-state is induced. This is one of the many explanations of the sleep and dream states.

All various theories agree that the *Sushumna* is closed at the bottom and that unless the breathing operation in *Ida* and *Pingala Nadis* is restrained, the *Sushumna* would not open up. This is true about the breath and the condition for the *Kundalini* to enter the *Sushumna* as life-energy. The *Jivatman* then follows the path of the life force exclusively through the *Sushumna* and on its path exist the higher worlds. But the *Jivatman's* mere contact with the tip of the *Sushumna* during sleep is different. When the body sleeps, a pseudo-*Samadhi* like state results.

The origins of the *Ida* and *Pingala Nadis* in the medulla cause involuntary respiration. In states of coma or unconsciousness, the origin point of *Ida* and *Pingala* stops releasing the normal degree of electrical impulses thus subduing the respiratory activity to the point of almost no breathing, which can result in death. Coma, unconsciousness and brain death are governed by subdued *Prana* or electrical impulses proceeding from the origin point of the *Ida* and *Pingala Nadis* inside the cerebro-spinal column on the *Sushumna Nadi*. In brain death, this centre continues to send electrical impulses thus causing mild respiration mechanically, but in that state, the *Jivatman* may have already left the body. Seemingly the body is living but without the real man inside.

Such a state is possible in brain death or irreversible coma in ordinary life. Similar to this phenomenon, a Yogi can leave his body, to come back to it later by will, by keeping the respiratory centre active through organising a controlled release of *Pranic* impulses from the origin point of *Ida* and *Pingala* on the *Sushumna Nadi*. The body thus goes on functioning, like the idling state of a motor engine in a car without the clutch being engaged.

In all states of the human being, the dormant *Kundalini* that lies coiled round the *Linga* three and half times in the *Muladhara* is linked to the *Sushumna*, making the body-consciousness uninterrupted. *Kundalini* is differently described as *Chit-Sakti* or pure consciousness, primal *Prakriti* or nature, and *Sabdabrahmamayi* or the cosmic sound of the *Sakti* that is the inseparable attribute of *Siva* when the manifest world exists and as the proximate cause of creation. It is unmoving in a latent state and becomes dynamic when aroused and awakened. It can then take the *Jivatman* to higher and subtler psychic states, separating him from body-consciousness and our earthly life through the path of the *Sushumna Nadi*. It is obvious, therefore, that when *Kundalini* is at rest in the *Muladhara*, the *Jiva* has the three natural states of living — wakeful, sleeping and the dream. In these three natural states, the *Jiva's* contact with *Muladhara* is through the *Ida* and *Pingala*.

When the *Kundalini* is awakened, the *Jivatman* can by effort enter into the fourth state in *Sushumna* known as *Turiya*. In the normal state, the *Sushumna* remains closed at its lower end and opens only when the *Kundalini* is awakened when the respiratory activity by *Ida* and *Pingala* is arrested. The two flanking channels of psychic energy *Ida* and *Pingala* on the left and right respectively are known as 'white *Chandra* or moon' and 'red *Surya* or sun'. The *Sushumna* and these two *Nadis* ultimately unite at the forehead-centre.

If, by effort, the *Kundalini* is made to disengage from the *Linga*, it travels upwards along the *Sushumna Nadi* to the brain-centre in great speed without stopping anywhere. Yet it does not stay put at the brain-centre either, but quickly comes back to *Muladhara* only to coil itself round the *Linga* once again. By repeated attempts, the Yogi arouses the *Kundalini* from its deep slumber, and by exercising a control over it, fixes it at one of the six centres, which are like stations on the railway line. Just as a station is the gateway to a city, each centre or chakra is a gateway to a *Loka*, a separate world.

The Yogi's *Jivatman* can enter such worlds by piercing the centres at will and lastly can leave the body through piercing the crown of the head. That would take him to *Brahma Loka*. In the case of ordinary men, at the time of leaving the body, the *Jivatman* must return to the *Muladhara*. Death occurs, as already described, by the withdrawal of all *Pranas* to the heart-centre, thus switching off all the centers, **making it no longer possible for the *Jivatman* to move. This results in the pain of death, which is not comparable to any other pain in life.** The three *Nadis* are also switched off forcing the *Jivatman* out of the body.

The *Yoga Sastra* has devised ways and means to keep the electrical lifeline of the *Nadi* network going and yet allow the soul leave the body voluntarily. By virtue of this, a Yogi can reenter his body or enter into another body with or without a soul in it. This is known as *Parakaya Pravesa Vidya*. This is a complex practice, and for us, it is only of theoretical but scientific interest.

7.2 Parakaya Pravesa Vidya (Knowledge of entering another body)

In the *Agamas* and Yogic texts and stories, *Parakaya Vidya*, the knowledge how to enter into the body of another person, has been briefly described. Being a secret science and also a risky practice, it should be taken up only in the presence of a competent Guru under his direct supervision. Its precise details have not been given by the authors in any texts. The *Agamas* describe how a Yogi can slowly come out of his own body and enter into another freshly dead body or a living human being. (This is another achievement of *Nachiketa Vidya*). The procedure briefly is as follows. The Yogi can perform the feat of *Parakaya Pravesa Vidya* like this:

In a secluded spot, assuming *Padmasana* while lying on his back on the ground (or floor) with a concentrated mind, he enters into the *Svadhisthana Agni* with his consciousness. He takes half of its life-energy with him, leaving half behind. After reaching the *Anaahata* or heart-centre, he makes a circumambulation three times around it with devotion to the Sun-like light at its centre. At this point of time, the Yogi becomes a *Hamsa*, the literal meaning of which is the divine-swan, but in fact, he achieves the consciousness of the Sun god. Then he chooses either the *Ida* or *Pingala Nadi* to go upwards. He reaches a point below the *Ajna Chakra*, touches the *Ajna Chakra* gently, comes down a little and exits the body through his nostrils.

He is free to go anywhere in space, but to make sure that he has mastered the art, he reenters his body through the *Muladhara* or the nostrils and repeats the exercise several times. After this mastery is achieved, he can travel in space and also appear before people, activating his own sense of vision anywhere. In fact, even in ordinary human life there are cases when dead people, immediately after dying, make a hazy appearance to those dear to them at a distance. This is often called an apparition, but it is actually the departed soul.

In this phenomenon, the six-petalled Lotus of the *Svadhisthana* plays a vital role. The six petals contain the sounds — *Bam*, *Bham*, *Mam*, *Yam*, *Ram* and *Lam*. Those who do *Sadhana* on this chakra can destroy *Kama* (desire), *Krodha* (anger), *Mada* (intoxication) and *Matsarya* (jealousy), which are responsible for the man committing various sins that lead to hell-like experiences. In the *Parakaya Vidya*, the qualification for the Yogi is that he must have conquered these elements within him and be free from unrighteous desires.

If such weaknesses remain in him, it would be impossible for him to reenter his own body.

The question here arises as to how he can enter into a dead body in which the flow of the life energy from the brain to the *Muladhara* was already switched off once and for all at the time of the soul's departure. We have seen that the function of breathing, dependent on the *Ida* and *Pingala Nadis* being active, is a compulsory condition for a *Jiva* to function in a body. We have also noted that when a Yogi leaves his body he keeps it alive for him to reenter on his return. This means that *Ida* and *Pingala Nadis* in his body are left functioning while his consciousness is away.

The doubt arises, whether life can be rekindled in a dead body by the Yogi who enters into and if so by what process? The *Jivatman*, it should be understood, actually rekindles the extinguished fire in the dead body and restarts the life-process. This is possible for the Yogi by taking the element of fire with him when he goes out of his body. This element in the body resides in *Svadhisthana* plexus. Actually the *Muladhara*, *Svadhisthana* and *Manipura*, the three lower *chakras*, are all primarily governed by the fire element upon which their respective elements, the earthy, fiery and watery elements are superimposed as secondary principles.

The Yogi, as *Angustha Purusha*, enters into the dead body through the *Apana Marga* (path) in most cases, through the downward-moving *Vayu*. He can also enter through the nasal path, but then it is said to be more difficult to kindle the fire first. *Svadhisthana* being closer to *Muladhara*, he kindles the fire in *Svadhisthana* as a result of which the *Apana Prana* at *Muladhara*, *Samana Prana* at the navel-centre, *Udana Prana* at the throat-centre, and ultimately the *Mukhya Prana* at the heart-centre come back to life in quick succession. The respiratory function can then start. *Ida* and *Pingala* are reestablished in their movements. The brain cells are partly brought to life as the original ego had left and the ego of the

Yogi is introduced in its place. The Yogi, thus, uses the dead body as a functional tool with his own ego working in it.

All this is mentioned here only to describe the achievements of Yogic science (*Yoga Sastra*). The great achievement of the Yogi is his ability to enter or leave his body at will as an individual intact. The secret behind this ability is that he is capable of entering into and riding on the fire element that pervades the whole creation, filling the entire space, including that inside the human body. This capacity is exclusive to the fire element. It is for this reason that the *Aryans* worshipped Fire in their *Yajnas* and were able to send their offerings through fire to the Gods in any *Loka.*

Fire, therefore, is the best carrier of the essence of matter, or a *Jiva* or a message from one world to another. The Yogi, leaving his body, enters into the fiery element of the worlds and goes anywhere in space, including to the other *Lokas*. For this reason, *Agni* is called the *Duta* or messenger (*Agnim dootam vrineemahe....*).

The same messenger *Agni*, therefore, should be used as a vehicle for travel in space by the *Jivatman*. Even in the final merger in the supreme *Brahman*, *Agni Upasana* (meditative worship of fire) can merge the *Jivatman* into itself (*Agni*) and universalise the soul. This is like how a small crystal of salt, entering into a pot of water, can pervade the whole pot. Whether for achieving the grace of the higher worlds for material benefits here, for reaching the higher worlds themselves, or for the ultimate merger in the fire element pervading the universe, *Agni* can always be approached. The entire religion of the *Aryans* is centered around the discovery of this great universal truth of *Agni*. In Yoga too, the same secret works wonders.

In the ordinary cases of Yoga *Sadhakas*, the pericarp or top of the brain is usually chosen for leaving the body at death. Such a departure is believed to afford the soul entry into the higher worlds. This pericarp is the *Sahasrara* or thousand-petalled Lotus, at the centre of which the primordial dual-principle, 'the male and the female' or *Siva* and *Parvati* who reside there in a united state. A soul that reaches this point and gains release from there conquers the sense of duality forever. The *Jiva* leaves *Prakriti* forever, and is no more an enjoyer of nature, which is the liberation from all bondage.

7.3 Breath Control or *Pranayama*

In connection with this Yoga, a few words about *Pranayama* are relevant, taking ideas from the special *Upanishads* related to Yoga. First some facts should be noted as follows. The *Pingala Nadi* is approached through the right nostril and *Ida Nadi* through the left nostril. The *Nadis* are totally tamed and brought under control through the practice of *Pranayama*. Inhalation, retention and exhalation should be done through the same *Nadi* repeatedly and the period of retention should be gradually increased over a time.

Ultimately, retention can be practiced for about sixty seconds or one minute at a time. When the retention capability approaches sixty seconds, inhalation through the *Ida* and exhalation through *Pingala* should be performed. At this stage once again, after exhalation through *Pingala*, inhalation should be practiced only through *Pingala Nadi*. The time of inhalation through *Pingala* should be thirty seconds. Four times a day, the practice must be kept regular for three months.

Ultimately a Yogi attains a capacity to retain his breath without any inhalation and exhalation noticeably occurring. *Kumbhaka Siddhi* or retention control is achieved when profuse sweating and shaking of the body occurs with a heating-up of the skin. This can be followed by levitation or other *Siddhis* in due course. Immense strength of the body follows if the discipline is maintained along with celibacy.

When retention of the breath is achieved without inhalation or exhalation, the breath enters into the *Sushumna* voluntarily. This is the stage for starting the *Pranava Upasana* or practice of *Om* in the extended or *Pluta* form (three *Matras*). Over a time, *Pranava* destroys all obstacles in practice. A state known as *Ghata Avastha* is ultimately reached when *Prana* and *Apana*, *Manas* and *Buddhi*, *Jivatman* and *Paramatman* become one and balanced, losing their differentiated states. At this stage, the *Kumbhaka* (retention) practice need be done only once a day (one sitting for 30 or 40 minutes). All the senses of the body should be then treated as the *Atman*, and the eight *Siddhis* together with the ability to move in the sky can follow at any time depending upon various factors. But these should be ignored or they can become obstacles along the path.

By the several stages that follow, a Yogi reaches '*Brahma Jnana*'. Many secrets are taught in the *Yoga Upanishads* like *Yoga*, *Kshurika*, *Brahma*, *Mandala Brahmana* and so on, in the name of *Amanaska Yoga*, *Sabija Samadhi*, *Nirbija Samadhi* and other topics. These should be practiced under the guidance of a competent Guru. The technical particulars of practicing *Om* have been explained earlier.

7.4 *Anaahata* and bodily states

As explained earlier, the *Angustha Purusha* or inch-man dwells close to the heart-centre, moving up and down while ruling over the body through the senses and *Pranas* while the *Ida* and *Pingala nadis* are functioning. He enters *Sushumna* exclusively by Yogic practice, and he may consider his goal as the form of *Siva* or *Narayana* or the void inside the Heart. Through the power of the *Sushumna Nadi*, the *Jivatman* loses its identity with the live human being or the mortal body-state.

Once entry and exclusive movement in *Sushumna* is achieved, the phenomenal world for the man disappears or sleeps. The very name '*Sushumna*' indicates and implies '*Sushupti*' or sleep with reference to the phenomenal world. He awakens to the world of his choice. At this stage the various experiences of different Yogis are not uniform and vary from man to man.

Generally however, with reference to this world, the states should be known as follows, when subtle body is outside *Sushumna* and when it is in contact with *Muladhara* through *Ida* and *Pingala*. According to some traditions, when the *Jivatman* is placed at the eye-level, wakeful-state is obtained; at the throat-level, dream state; and deep sleep at the heart-level. When a deliberate meditation is directed toward super-human subjects like God, higher worlds etc., while in normal body consciousness the *Jivatman* can achieve these. In the ordinary dream state, the inner man may be running or riding etc., while the physical body lies motionless. Due to the actual physical non-involvement of the body, such an activity has become false and is being called a dream. In the human world, we consider that an activity is real only when the physical body is also involved. These various states are indicative of the various positions of *Jivaahamkaara* or the individual ego.

Inside the *Sushumna* while in the Yogic-state, a Yogi can also come to a lower world attention (barring dream) by reaching the eye level in the head, since he is in *Samadhi* by staying near the heart-centre. *Sushumna* is the path on which he moves up and down. *Kundalini* is the energy with the help of which a Yogi moves through the *Brahma Nadi* or *Sushumna Nadi*. To repeat again, entry into the *Brahma Nadi* is possible through the awakening of the *Kundalini*, the central energy line.

The ultimate goal of Yogi is to identify his self with the *Atman* or *Brahman*, in which state all world consciousness is crossed. In *Savikalpa Samadhi* (*Samadhi* with awareness), the knower and the known exist separately but experience is gone through by the self. In *Nirvikalpa Samadhi*, (*Samadhi* without awareness) the experiencer merges into the experience as the functioning of the ego ceases. But this is not the sleep-state, because in sleep there is no experience of any kind. Here in *Samadhi* there is a definite experience. The practice of Yoga leading one into the *Anaahata*-centre with the help of *Pranava* takes the Yogi into the ultimate *Samadhi* by stages. The Yogi is then one with the *Atman*, who is the witness to the three states of waking, sleep and dream.

7.5 Significance of the name *Katha:* the Heart-centre of the *Upanishad*

We have elsewhere said that the *Ida* and *Pingala Nadis* closely cross over the central *Sushumna* creating a junction point. They do so at three alternate centres — *Svadhisthana*, *Anaahata* and *Ajna* - called *Granthis* named after *Brahma*, *Vishnu* and *Rudra*.

In physical anatomy, the *Anaahata Chakra* corresponds to cardio-plexus. Among the *Lokas* it corresponds to *Maharloka*. This chakra on the *Sushumna* emanates a deep red light. At its centre is a dark region circumscribed by a hexagon. This hexagon is *Vayu Mandala* or the windy region. Outside it, there is *Surya Mandala* or the sphere of the Sun, with a triangle lustrous as million lightnings inside it. Outside this, is the surrounding heart-lotus of twelve petals, emanating a red light. These concentric regions in the *chakra* are governed by different deities like *Kakini* and *Rudra*. (When we reach the subtle stages representing the higher worlds, we are governed by the deities or divinities of these respective worlds.) *Vayu Bija 'Yam'* rules the peripheral region. The letters on the petals are not as though written on the physical petals of a lotus. They are sounds one can hear while meditating on the petals one by one while in a near *Samadhi*. Every letter, thus heard, grants miraculous powers to the Yogi.

Anaahata is the fourth *chakra* from below close below which is the divine '*Kalpa Vriksha*' (wish-fulfilling tree) also known as *Ananda kanda* or the region of bliss. This is a minor centre below the *Anaahata*. The *Anaahata* is of *Vayu Tattva* (wind element). A sound (cosmic hiss) is heard at this centre. Wind is responsible for the propagation of sound. In *Anaahata*, the wind element carries not any caused sound but the primordial *Nada*, the hum identified as *Pranava*, which is self-revealing. This *Pranava* pervades the wind and sky in

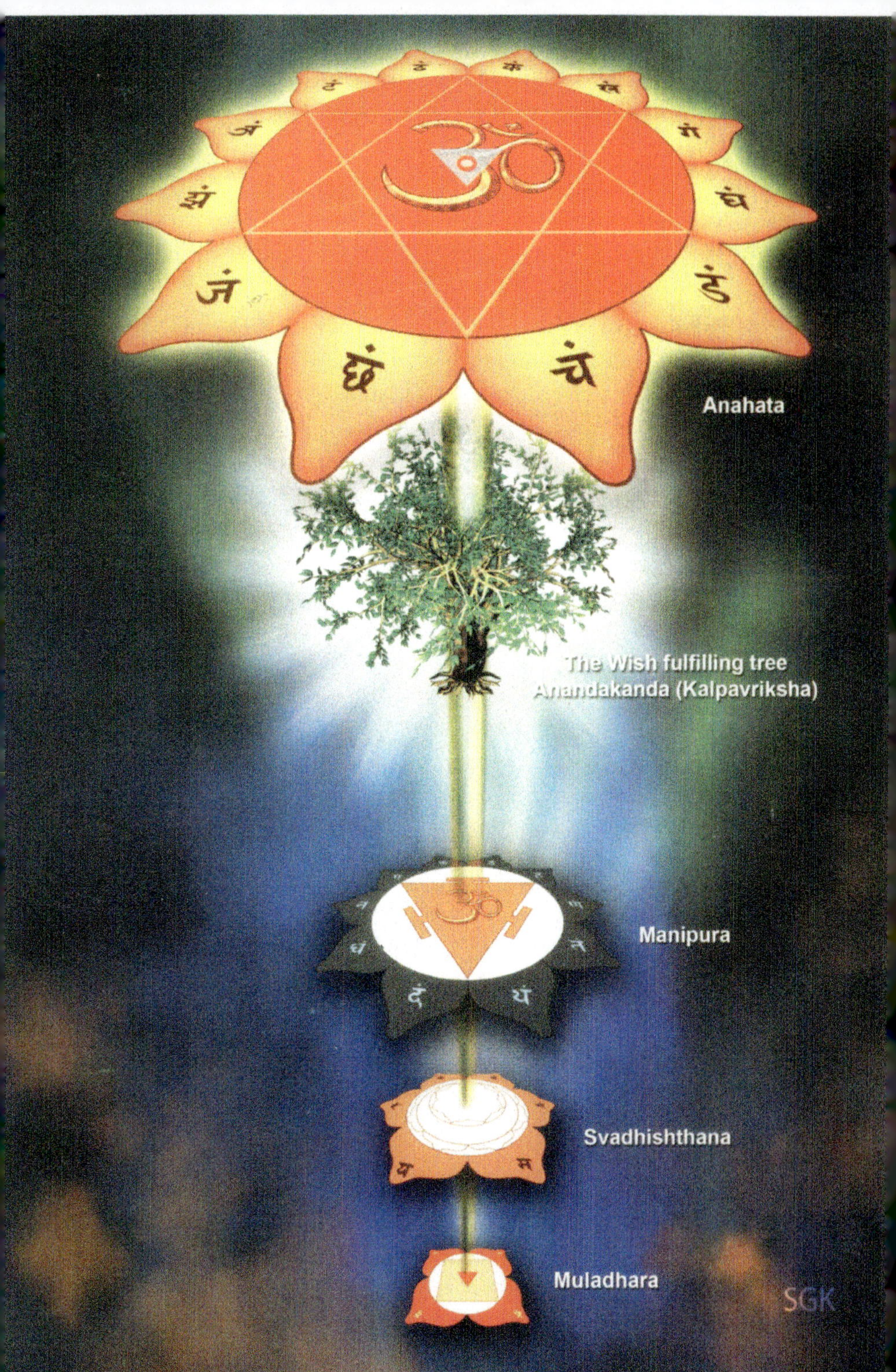

The placement of Anandakanda, the Wish flfillment Kalpavriksha, which the puranas describe as being placed in swaraga or heaven. This is an enticing obstacle to liberation - significantly placed at the threshold of the entry into the ultimate Anahata

the creation. The element of the *chakra* being wind, and the region of darkness inside being absolute void (*Akasa*), *Pranava* is heard from within.

For this reason, one who takes *Pranava* as his vehicle reaches the *Dahara Akasa* or heart-space easily because he has attuned himself to it by *Pranava*. In his penetration into the chakra, he takes the help of the presiding deities *Isana* or *Rudra* and his *Sakti*, *Kakini*. The outer peripheral petals are to be meditated upon as shining reddish yellow in colour and vermilion alternately. *Kakini* holds a skull in one hand and *Pasa* (the rope) in the other hand, indicating the cessation of births. The related literature should be carefully studied by the Yogi.

Where is the place of the *Mukhya Prana*? *Anaahata* is elsewhere described as the seat of the *Samskaras*, the tendencies and *Gunas* of past existences in *Prakriti*, which is why man's proximity to it in living releases the results of Karma. It is the seat of desires, bodily ego, *Manas*, *Buddhi* and *Chitta* (mind, intellect and consciousness). Instead of the *Jiva* unsteadily living in its proximity while *Ida* and *Pingala* are functioning with the accompanying body-consciousness, if this normal state of man is suspended by the full entry of the *Prana* into the *Sushumna* and the *Jivatman* following it, the Yogi can reach the lotus formed by the combination of the three *Nadis* — *Ida*, *Pingala* and *Sushumna*. Then he can enter into the *Anaahata* by penetrating through the outer, powerful wind-current; propitiating the wind-element with the *Bija mantra* '*Yam*'.

Here, in *Raja Yoga*, the Yogi is directed to visualise *Siva* and *Sakti* in a dual state. In fact, the *Raja Yoga* maintains the *Siva-Sakti* duality even in *Sahasrara*, though in an inseparable condition. In the same tradition, even in *Anaahata*, *Siva* and *Sakti* are approached with a sense of duality.

However, the way shown by the Katha Upanishad is that *Anaahata* is entered into through the *Vayu Mandala*. Instead of reaching the *Purusha-Prakriti* dual (but inseparable) presence in the pericarp, the primordial fundamental truth is realised through the meditation on *Om*. *Anaahata*, as the very name indicates, is the place of the 'Universal *Nada*' which is the source of all excited sounds. The *Anaahata Nada* that is universal is like the permanent ocean, while sound created by any other means is short-lived, like the wave in the ocean, caused by the wind, boat or other factors. Whatever sound is caused artificially is fleeting and soon disappears into the permanent ocean of the 'Universal *Nada*'. That *Nada* can be heard when one enters into the heart-centre leaving behind the phenomenal 'word/meaning duality' of the material world.

The pure *Nada* inside the space of the *Anaahata* is '*Omkara*' which is *Isvara* himself, as asserted by the *Yoga Sastra* in the words, *'Tasya Vaachakah Pranavah'*. Whatever be Yoga's concept of the *Isvara* that governs the Universe, it is defined as the *Pranava Nada* present in the heart-centre. Thus, hearing this *Nada* in the heart-centre is experiencing God while in *Samadhi*. Ultimately, *Jivatman* can merge with this *Paramatman* present as *Nada* in the *Anaahata*.

The Lord of Death addresses the *Angustha Purusha* of Nachiketa while the latter is away from his physical body, directly granting him the secret of absorption into the supreme *Brahman*. Nachiketa has to go back to his physical body on earth as desired by him, and yet attains liberation by this means of *Nada Yoga*.

The twelve petals of the *Anaahata* hold the *Bijaksharas* — *Kam*, *Kham*, *Gam*, *Gham*, *Jnyam*, *Cham*, *Chham*, *Jam*, *Jham*, *Nyam*, *Tam* and *Tham* — beginning with *Kam* and ending with *Tham*. The name derived is *KATHA* meaning all the secrets contained between these two *Bijas* (sounds), are explained therein. There are many more secrets. It is not possible to reveal or even to reasonably explain them all. Only one who takes the pains to go through the basic and gradually advancing Yoga practice of the *Anaahata* will gain a direct experience of it; after which the reading of the *Upanishad* makes it more meaningful, simple and direct in its import.

Such knowledge can be imparted by a Guru, only to a genuine disciple. This last revelation about its name is sufficient to accept that the *Upanishad* is a '*Yoga Upanishad*'. Discerning readers well-versed and initiated into Yoga can certainly go into its secret treasure of more revelations.

There is also a tradition that traces the name *KATHA* to the name of a Rishi, after whom '*Kathaka*' is given as the name of the relevant portion of the *Veda*.

Patanjali's Yoga Sutras also mentions the *chakras*. In '*Vibhuti Pada*', the *Siddhis* or achievements of concentration or *Samyamana* on various chakras are described. *Samyamana* means *Dhyana*, *Dharana* and *Samadhi* which mean absolute concentrated dwelling on the *Chakra* through the *Sushumna*. The achievements like *Parakaya Vidya* or entering another body, dead or alive, and the ability to see higher *Lokas* are described. *Samyamana* on the *Atman* leads to *Moksha*. The *Chitta* or consciousness is the means of such achievements in *Patanjali's Sutras*. The *Siddhis* described are *Jyotismati*, *Madhumati* and so on.

7.6 Sri Gorakshanath: The Great Guru of Yoga

In the world of *Maha Yogis*, *Sri Gorakshanath*, popularly known as '*Gorakh*', occupies the supreme position commanding an unequalled status of a divinity on earth. He is acknowledged as an incarnation of *Rudra* or *Siva* himself. Yoga being a means of dissolving the ego into the Unlimited and *Rudra* being the god of the dissolution of the Creation into *Brahman*, *Rudra* referred to as *Siva* is the ultimate goal for the Yogi inside himself. *Rudra*, being one of the trinity of great Gods, is the starting point for crossing the state of bondage. Transcending the principles of 'Creation' and 'Sustenance' governed by *Brahma* and *Vishnu*; the Yogi reaches the ends of Creation. Crossing the manifest creation, the Yogi finds himself at the threshold of the primordial duality at its origin, the *Purusha* and *Prakriti* known as *Siva* and *Sakti*.

The Yogi, who travels from *Muladhara* upwards, reaches the *Brahmarandhra*, leaving behind him all the manifest creation. Reaching that spot, the Yogi finds himself ready for absorption. The nature in him, called '*Prakriti*', is merged into the *Sakti* when the remaining unqualified soul in him is absorbed into the *Brahman.* This is the ultimate release.

Having reached that penultimate state, the Yogi, 'who has by then conquered all ignorance and achieved the status of God himself in his own finite self ' is then capable of reaching or living in any superior world at will and helping seekers trapped in ignorance below. *Sri Gorakhnath* has such a status, remaining as a guru in the higher worlds that seekers on earth can call on.

'*Goraksha Sataka*' and '*Goraksha Vachana Sangraha*' are part of the literature ascribed to him. The path he teaches chiefly consists of the *Kundalini Yoga* but according to the principles of *Advaita*. The path existed even long before *Sri Krishna* and is known as the '*Gorakh Panth*'.

Patanjali's '*Yoga Sastra*' is a treatise on the philosophy of Yoga. *Hatha Yoga* should be treated as a supplementary and complimentary manual of detailed instruction. '*Gorakh Panth*' can be regarded as to having been in vogue prior to these great works, linking their contents with a tradition of untraceable times of yore. The personality of *Gorakhnath*, covering an unlimited span of time up to the present, provides a living proof of the antiquity of Yoga.

This path of *Gorakh* takes its base in the theory '*Dvaitadvaita lakshanam paramatattvam*' — the 'duality cum non duality state' of the ultimate truth. The *Sadhana* consists of all the *Yoga Chakras*. The teachings of the *Upanishads* and Vedanta are also accepted with the assertion that *Siva* himself being the soul is the truth to be realised for *Moksha*.

* * * * *

Part II
THE KATHA-UPANISHAD

A General Commentary on Vallis I to III

OM SAHA NAAVAVATU
SAHA NAU BHUNAKTU
SAHA VEERYAM KARAVAAVAHAI
TEJASVI NAAVADHEETAMASTHU
MAAVIDVISAAVAHAI
OM SANTIH SANTIH SANTIH

First Section — PRATHAMA VALLI

Om Namo bhagavate Vaivasvataaya mrityave brahmavidyaachaaryaaya Nachiketase cha

1. *Om Usanha vai Vaajasravasah sarvavedasam dadau Tasya ha Nachiketaa naama putra aasa*

Salutations to God of Death, the teacher of the *Brahma Vidya* to Nachiketa! Once, *Vajasravasa* gave all his wealth away for a sacrifice. He had a son, Nachiketa by name.

2. *Tagm ha kumaaragm santam dakshinaasu Neeyamaanaasu sraddhaavivesa somanyata*

While the gifts were being offered by his father to the *Brahmins*, an attention entered into Nachiketa, though still a child. He thought....

3. *Peetodakaa jagdhatrinaa dugdhadohaa nirindriyaah Anandaanaama te lokaastaan sa gacchati taa dadat*

One who gives away in charity such cows that have already drunk their water and eaten their grass, that are emptied of milk and whose organs have no strength, he goes to those worlds known as joyless (a-nanda).

4. *Sa hovaacha pitaram tata kasmai maam daasyaseeti Dviteeyam triteeyam tagm ho vaacha mrityave tvaa dadaameeti*

Nachiketa asked his father, "Father! To whom will you offer me?" He repeated this question a second and a third time. To him his father said, "I give you to Death."

Commentary:

This question probably arose in the mind of Nachiketa, apart from destiny, by his curiosity that useless cattle were mixed among those that were being given away and so the charity would be tainted. Seeing this, a deep faith entered in him to fulfill his father's sacrifice. This could be perhaps corrected by himself being given away.

5. *Bahoonaamemi prathamo bahoonaamemi madhyamah*
Kigm svidyamasya kartavyam yanmayaadya karisyati

Nachiketa replied: I go as the first among many, as also in the midst of many. Then what is Yama's (the God of Death's) purpose (that he will do) with me now?

Commentary:

Since he knows all people die anyway, Nachiketa wonders what special purpose Yama might have with him. Another interpretation is that if animals are sacrificed in the *Yaga* in the name of the Gods according to Vedic injunctions, what could be the principle behind himself, a boy, being offered as part of the same *Yajna*? In other words, was it part of charity or was it a sacrifice in the *Yajna*?

6. *Anupasya yathaa poorve pratipasya tathaa pare*
Sasyamiva martyah pachyate sasyamivaa jaayate punah

See, just as those who have gone before, and reflect, just as those to come later; man grows and ripens like corn and is cut down like corn only to be born again.

Commentary:

Growth and death are part of the law of nature, whether it is for plants, animals or human beings. Yet while crops are useful to men, of what use is the death of human beings for God of Death? Why then should humans be killed by him?

7. *Vaisvaanarah pravisati atithirbraahmano grihaan*
Tasyaitaagm saantim kurvanti hara Vaivasvatodakam

A *Brahmin* guest enters the homes as the sacred

Vaisvanara-fire. Then the householders take care of him and attend to his needs. Oh Death, Son of the Sun, bring water for the guest

Commentary:

Nachiketa has now gone to the house of Death expecting, as a Brahmin, to be attended to and requests the God of Death to bring him water. The hunger of the guest is the sacred *Vaisvanara Agni*. In the *Gita*, the Lord has said, "*Aham Vaisvaanaro bhootvaa praaninaam dehamaasritah*" meaning "Becoming the *Vaisvanara* or digestive fire, I am placed in the bodies of all living beings." In feeding the guest, the Lord in the nature of *Vaisvanara Agni* is pleased by the food given.

These words could be those of Nachiketa reminding Yama of the significance of feeding the guest in the prescribed manner and asking for water or it could be asking for propitiation of the guest-god. A departed soul is offered water on earth, which Nachiketa was seeking from Yama. The last word, '*Udakam*' could even mean '*Vaivasvata Odanam*' meaning food (*Odanam*), fitting into the context of the Dharma of feeding the guest stated in the first line.

8. *Aaasaa prateekshe sangatagm soonritaam cha*
Istaapoorte putrapasoogmscha sarvaan
Etadvrinkte purusasyaalpamedhaso
Yasyaanasnan vasati braahmano grihe

If at anybody's household a *Brahmin* guest waits in expectation for food but is not cared for, all the merits of that foolish householder, whether from speaking the truth, sacrificial offerings, association with great men, or wealth of cattle and progeny will go to that guest himself.

Commentary:

Apart from his material wealth, the merit earned by "*Agnihotram, Tapas, Satyam, bhootaanaamcha anupaalanam, aatithyam, vaisvadevam cha*", worship of fire, meditation, truthfulness, kindness to living creatures, hospitality and the daily sacrifice of *Vaisvadevam* are the good deeds of a householder. These are lost if one does not have the adequate charity towards one's guests. These words can be taken as those of Nachiketa to Yama stating the Dharma. This statement implies that Lord Yama forfeited such wealth by the neglect of his guest.

9. *Tisro raatreeryadavaatseeh grihe me*
Anasnan brahmannatithirnamasyah
Namaste astu brahman svasti mestu
Tasmaatprati treen varaan vrineesva

Yama states: Oh *Brahmana*, salutations to you! You have stayed in my house for three nights as my guest, without eating. Therefore, ask three boons to correct this fault of mine, and let well being accrue to me.

10. *Saantasankalpah sumanaa yathaa syat*
Veetamanyuh Gautamo maabhi mrityo
Tvat prasristham maabhivadetprateeta
Etattrayaanaam prathamam varam vrine

Nachiketa replied: Oh Death! I ask as the first of the three boons that *Gautama* (my father) may be freed from anger towards me, may be peaceful with a clear mind, and that he may recognise and speak to me when you send me back home.

Commentary:

Since Nachiketa had actually not died, he could go back to the earth. Hence he requested reconciliation with his father. The boon was given.

11. *Yathaa purastaadbhavitaa prateeta*
Auddaalakiraarunih matprasristhah
Sukhagm raatreeh sayitaa veetamanyuh
Tvaam dadrusivaan mrityu mukhaatpramuktam

Yama replied: By recognising you, your father *Auddalaki*

Aruni will again be very affectionate just as he used to be. Seeing you liberated from the mouth of death, he will forget his anger or sorrow and will sleep happily through the nights.

12. *Svarge loke na bhayam kimchanaasti*
Na tatra tvam na jarayaa bibheti
Ubhe teertvaa asanaayaapipaase
Sokaatigo modate svargaloke

Nachiketa said: In heaven (*Svarga Loka*), there is no trace of fear. Neither you (Death), nor old age exists there. Men, crossing over both hunger and thirst, having gone beyond all sorrow rejoice in *Svarga Loka* (heaven).

Commentary:

Nachiketa is describing the world of heaven where the God of Death does not enter. There, people can continue to live in happiness for a long period of time without fear of death or suffering. He wants to gain this as his second boon.

13. *Sa tvamagnigm svargyamadhyesi mrityo*
Prabroohi tagm sraddadhaanaaya mahyam
Svargalokaa amritatvam bhajanta
Etat dviteeyena vrine varena

Oh Death! As you are that very fire which is capable of taking us to heaven, explain that to me since I am full of attention and faith. The residents of heaven enjoy immortality. This I ask you as my second boon.

14. *Pra te braveemi tadu me nibodha*
Svargyamagnim Nachiketah prajaanan
Anantalokaapti matho pratisthaam
Viddhi tvametam nihitam guhaayaam

Yama said: Oh Nachiketa! I will tell you fully about the fire that takes one to heaven. Learn it from me with full attention. When known, it bestows one an unlimited time in the higher worlds and also their foundation. **Know that this fire has its abode in the cave of heart**.

Commentary:

The God of Death has offered to teach not only the ritual that can gain heaven but reminds Nachiketa that the same secret is contained in the heart of man. He has offered to teach him not only the way to heaven but its foundation in the supreme that also lies within us. The secret Yoga is suggested. **This** mantra **is very clear that the 'death-conquering secret' of Yoga was also revealed by Yama to Nachiketa.** Nachiketa's concern is about knowing the higher worlds as a means of approaching the supreme truth, not as an end in itself.

15. *Lokaadimagnim tamuvaacha tasmai*
Yaa istakaa yaavateervaa yathaa vaa
Sa chaapi tatpratyavadadyathoktam
Athaasya mrityuh punarevaaha tusthah

The Lord of Death taught Nachiketa the fire sacrifice that is the means for attainment of the higher worlds and the details of the number of bricks and the method of their arrangement. And Nachiketa repeated Yama's instructions back to him as he was told. Then Death, satisfied with him, spoke again.

16. *Tamabraveet preeyamaano mahaatmaa*
Varam tavehaadya dadaami bhooyah
Tavaiva naamna bhavitaayamagnih
Srinkaam chemaamaneka roopaam grihaana

Being pleased, Yama, the noble one, said to him, "Now I bestow another boon upon you that you have not sought. This *Agni* will henceforth be known by your name. Also receive this necklace of many forms (Yoga *Siddhis*)."

Commentary:

Apart from the details of the ritual, Yama also initiated Nachiketa into the secret inner path, implying: "Take this multiple gift containing the physical ritual as well as the Yogic path, through which you can obtain the pleasures of the earth, the heaven and the higher worlds, and the path beyond these as well. This secret is given to you". The 'necklace' is metaphoric of Yogic *Siddhis* or higher powers.

17. *Trinaachiketastribhiretya sandhim*
Trikarmakrittarati janmamrityoo
Brahmajajnam devameedyam viditvaa
Nichaayya maagm saantimatyantameti

One who performs this Nachiketa ritual three times, going beyond the three knots and performing the three *Karmas*, he crosses over birth and death. Gaining the knowledge of *Brahman*, the supreme God adorable, through discernment, he reaches the ultimate peace.

Commentary:

Along with the performance of the ritual, Nachiketa is told to follow the inner path of Yoga for achieving the higher worlds. The six Yogic *Chakras* form three knots called *Granthis* (or *Sandhis* here), as we have already discussed them to be.

Muladhara and *Svadhisthana* control the earthy and the fiery elements respectively, but together are known as the *Agni Khanda*, the region of fire. They are knotted together at the *Brahma granthi*. *Manipura* and *Anaahata* centres rule the watery and airy elements respectively, but together comprise *Surya Khanda*, the realm of the Sun. They are knotted together at *Vishnu granthi*. *Visuddha* and *Ajna* centres are the sky and the mind elements respectively, but together comprise the region of *Chandra Khanda*, the realm of the Moon. They are knotted together at the *Rudra granthi*.

The Yogi who pierces these *Granthis* after controlling the six centres, conquers the three gunas of *Rajas*, *Sattva* and *Tamas*. The text *Lalita Sahasranama*, which deals with the power of *Kundalini* as *Parasakti*, also mentions these *Sandhis*. Even there, the various *Devis* and the appropriate offerings to them in the outer ritual are described. The Yogi, conquering these three *Sandhis* and three *Gunas*, gains release from the three conditions of birth, growth and death governed by the three deities *Brahma*, *Vishnu* and *Rudra*. This is *Atyantika Mukti*, the ultimate release.

Yama has given Nachiketa the secret of the inner sacrifice or *Antaryaaga* through which the *Jivatman* breaks these knots and neutralises the causes of rebirth and death that exist within himself. He can achieve not only heaven as an outer world but the supreme inner heaven of the highest *Brahman* beyond the worlds.This Vedic ritual and the Yogic achievement have already been explained in the first section of this book.

18. *Trinaachiketastrayametat viditvaa*
Ya evam vidvaagm schinute Naachiketam
Sa mrityu paasan puratah pranodya
Sokaatigo modate svargaloke

One who performs this Nachiketa ritual three times after having known these three secrets and thus knowingly builds the Nachiketa fire, destroying the bonds of death, he goes beyond all sorrow and rejoices in the world of heaven.

19. *Esha te agnirNachiketah svargyo*
Yamavrineethaa dviteeyena varena
Etamagnim tavaiva pravakshyanti janaasah
Triteeyam varam Nachiketo vrineesva

Yama says: Oh Nachiketa! This is your fire that leads to heaven, which you have chosen as your second boon. People will name this Agni after you. Now, ask for the third boon.

20. *Yeyam prete vichikitsaa manushye*
Asteetyeke naayamasteeti chaike
Etadvidyaa manusisthah tvayaaham
Varaanaamesha varastriteeyah

Nachiketa asked: There is a debate about the condition of the soul after the death of a man. Some say "It exists" and others, "It doesn't." I want your instruction about this, since I aspire to know it. I ask this as the third boon that you have granted me.

Commentary:

Nachiketa, like all mortals, is in the dark about what transcends death. In fact, he is not in his body on earth, but in his subtle body. Yet this itself is not sufficient to understand the condition of all *Jivas* who are dying, and hence the question. Nachiketa is not simply content with knowing that he can gain heaven, the higher worlds in which there is freedom from death for a long period of time but not the final liberation, he wants to know the ultimate mystery of life and death; which is secret of creation.

21. *Devairatraapi vichikitsitam puraa*
Na hi suvijneya manuresa dharmah
Anyam varam Nachiketo vrineesva
Maa moparotseerati maa srijainam

Yama replied: Nachiketa! Even the Gods before have had such doubts. This Dharma which is too subtle is not easy to understand for mere men. Not this, ask some other boon. Do not press me on it, relieve me from this obligation.

22. *Devairatraapi vichikitsitam kila*
Tvam cha mrityo yanna sujneya maattha
Vaktaa chaasya tvaadriganyo na labhyo
Naanyo varastulya etasya kaschit

Nachiketa replied: Even the Gods have had doubts about this and it is not easy to know as you yourself have described. Oh Death! You are the best teacher for this. There is no one else who is your equal (since you are the governing God of all souls after their death). No other boon could equal this one.

23. *Sataayusah putrapautraan vrineesva*
Bahoon pasoonhasti hiranya masvaan
Bhoomermahadaayatanam vrineesva
Svayam cha jeeva sarado yaavadicchasi

Yama said: Ask for sons and grandsons that live a hundred years. Ask for much cattle, elephants, gold and horses. Ask for a vast territory of land. And live for as many years as you desire.

24. *Etattulyam yadi manyase varam*
Vrineesva vittam chirajeevikaam cha
Mahaabhoomau Nachiketastvamedhi
Kaamaanaam tvaa kaamabhaajam karomi

Ask another boon that you consider equal to this. Ask for a very long life. Ask for all riches, ask for a large kingdom and rule over it. I will make you enjoy all the desires possible for a man.

25. *Ye ye kaamaa durlabhaa martyaloke*
Sarvaankaamaagm schandatah praarthayasva
Imaa raamaah sa rathaah sa toorya
Na heedrisaa lambhaneeyaa manushyaih
Aabhirmatprattabhih parichaarayasva
Nachiketo maranam maanupraakseeh

Those desires, which are very difficult to get in the mortal world, ask for any pleasing thing that you want. These beautiful women, chariots and horses that I offer are not like anything that men can gain. Receive such rewards from me, Nachiketa, but do not press me on the secret of death.

26. *Svobhaavaa martyasya yadantakaitat*
Sarvendriyaanaam jarayanti tejah
Api sarvam jeevita malpameva
Tavaiva vaahaastava nrityageete

Nachiketa replied: Oh Death! These mortal enjoyments have a quick end. They wear out the vigor of all the senses. Even with all these, life is short. Let them be with you; these horses, dancing and singing women and other enjoyments.

27. *Na vittena tarpaneeyo manusyo*
Lapsyaamahe vittamadraakshma chettvaa
Jeevisyaamo yaavadeesisyasi tvam
Varastu me varaneeyah sa eva

Whatever the wealth he may gain, man is not content. Let us gain, see and sacrifice whatever wealth we gain. Let us live as long as you wish us to live. I insist upon that same boon about death, which I have asked from you.

28. *Ajeeryataamamritaanaamupetya*
Jeeryanmartyah kvadhah sthah prajaanan
Abhidhyaayan varnaratipramodaan
Ati deerghe jeevite ko rameta

Having reached immortals like you who are imperishable and having known them, an aging mortal aware of his inferior existence, considering the enjoyments of the body and senses, how could he want to enjoy them even during a very long life?
Commentary:
Having seen death and through it gotten a sense of the higher meaning of life, it is not possible for a person to return to the enjoyments of ordinary life and be satisfied with them. This is *Vairagya*, freedom from desires.

29. *Yasminnidam vichikitsanti mrityo*
Yatsaamparaaye mahati broohi nastat
Yo ayam varo goodha manupravistho
Naanyam tasmaanNachiketaa vrineete

Oh Death! Teach us that secret about which even the Gods inquire; which allows for the great transition beyond death. Apart from this boon about the secret truth, I, Nachiketa do not choose any other.
Commentary:
The detachment and renunciation of Nachiketa has been tested and found complete. This is a pre-condition to the

higher knowledge. One cannot know the truth about death without oneself being willing to die, which means be willing to forego all the enjoyments of not only of physical life but of heaven afterwards.

* * *

Second Section — DVITEEYA VALLI

1. *Anyachchreyo anyadutaiva preya*
Ste ubhe naanaarthe purushagm sineetah
Tayoh sreya aadadaanasya saadhu bhavati
Heeyate arthaadya vu preyo vrineete

Yama speaks: Different indeed is what is good (*Sreyas*) and different what is pleasing in the material world (*Preyas*). Reaching different goals, all men are bound by one of these two. Those who have chosen the good become immortal while the others seeking only what is pleasing fall from the goal of liberation.

2. *Sreyascha preyascha manusyameta*
Stau sampareetya vivinakti dheerah
Sreyo hi dheero abhi preyaso vrineete
Preyo mando yogakshemaadvrineete

Man in this world is confronted with both the ultimate-good and with the materialistic pleasures. The courageous man keenly examines both with sharp discrimination and chooses the good. The unwise prefer only what is pleasing, seeking only their own welfare and security.

3. *Sa tvam priyaanpriyaroopaagmscha kaamaa*
Nabhidhyaayan Nachiketo atyasraaksheeh
Naitaagm srinkaam vittamayee mavaapto
Yasyaam majjanti bahavo manusyah

Oh Nachiketa! After deep consideration, you have discarded all the desires and objects of desires in this world.

You have not fallen into this golden trap of wealth, in which many men have sunk.

Commentary:

The Guru, the God of Death, is satisfied with the renunciation of Nachiketa and appreciates him for it. Nachiketa has avoided the trap of desire, material gain and enjoyment that is the main goal of all people born. As these states are bound by death, by rejecting them, he is now fit to be taught by the God of Death about the secrets of immortality.

4. *Dooramete vipareete visoochee*
Avidyaa yaa cha vidyeti jnaataa
Vidyaabheepsinam Nachiketasam manye
Na tvaa kaamaa bahavo alolupanta

Wisdom (*Vidya*) and ignorance (*Avidya*) are distant from one another. They move in contrary paths that go in opposite directions. I consider Nachiketa to be a true aspirant for wisdom who is not lured by the many desires of the world.

Commentary:

Here God is describing the common man's ignorance. The God acknowledges Nachiketa's quality and his firm desire for knowledge.

5. *Avidyaayaamantare vartamaanaah*
Svayam dheeraah panditammanyamaanaah
Dandramyamaanaah pariyanti moodhaa
Andhenaiva neeyamaanaa yathaandhaah

While living in ignorance, men believe that they themselves are wise and learned. Like drunkards who are imbalanced, such foolish men wander in confusion like the blind leading the blind.

Commentary:

This verse relates to so-called teachers who themselves are ignorant. They are like the blind leading the blind. The paths taught by such so-called wise men revolve around mere action (*karma*) or mere theoretical discourses and can never lead one to renunciation or true knowledge. The intellectual pride of men about this knowledge of spiritual search is also condemned by God. The followers of such men also are led blindly to no real goal. They never get beyond the net of words and ideas. This *mantra* is also found in the *Mundaka Upanishad* (1-2-8).

6. *Na saamparaayah pratibhaati baalam*
Pramaadyantam vittamohena moodham
Ayam loko naasti para iti maanee
Punah punarvasamaapadyate me

Like one who is caught in dangers due to greed for money, the fool has no sense of the after-life future in his mind. Men who believe that there is nothing else except this world are coming into my hold (the grip of death) again and again.

Commentary:

The ignorance of men is again described. People do not think of the distant future beyond death. Their thoughts are limited to their future joys and sorrows in this world only. Such people only meet their inevitable end, repeatedly, and do not profit from the experience of life.

7. *Sravanaayaapi bahubhiryo na labhyah*
Srinvantopi bahavo yam na vidyuh
Aascharyo vaktaa kusalo asya labdhaa
Aascharyo jnaataa kusalaanusisthah

Much intellectual explanation and even much listening to such teaching does not grant the experience of the Truth. Rare are those who have taught it and equally rare are those who have learnt it. Such a man who could give such a teaching and one who experienced it at his heart (by taking this teaching inside) are a (rare) wonder indeed.

Commentary:

Any amount of mere study or discourse cannot reveal the secret of what transcends death. He is indeed a wonder who is so wise as to be benefited by mere teaching!

8. *Na narenaavarena prokta esa*
Suvijneyo bahudhaa chintyamaanah
Ananyaprokte gatiratra naasti
Aneeyaanhyatarkyam anupramaanaat

This (the *atma* or *Brahman*), when described by a commoner (or an ignorant man) is expressed and explained in many ways. It is neither understood easily nor has it any other means of expression than that of man. It is subtle like an atom, even subtler than it, totally beyond grasp and is beyond all logical interpretation or exposition.

Commentary:

Taught by an incompetent human being, whose mind still has many doubts, this secret is expressed in a confusing or contradictory manner. Yet unless taught by another, a truly great teacher, the real secret cannot be imparted. There is no way of reaching the goal otherwise, but when properly taught and followed, there is no travel involved from one place to another. The goal is reached here and now within oneself. The need of a true teacher is stressed here (which is rare), while pointing out the futility of an unrealised teacher (of which there are always many).

9. *Naishaa tarkena matiraapaneya*
Proktaa anyenaiva sujnaanaaya prestha
Yaam tvamaapah satyadhritirbataasi
Tvaa drikjno bhooyaanNachiketah prasthaah

Dear Nachiketa! This secret knowledge is not obtained by means of any intellectual, logical discussion or interpretation. It is realised only when **imparted** by a Guru. You have come to me with a fully attentive mind and strong determination so that you have indeed achieved it. May we (the Gods or teachers) find more seekers of your kind!

Commentary:

There is no intellectual discussion possible about this deep secret. When a true *Jnani* teaches, his experience is shared even without the need of intellectual understanding. It goes directly to the heart. That is why a few great teachers could teach and awaken disciples through silence alone.

10. *Jaanaamyahagm sevadhirityanityam*
Na hyadhruvaih praapyate hi dhruvam tat
Tato mayaa Naachiketaschito agni
Ranityaih dravyaih praaptavaanasmi nityam

This body is ephemeral in nature like material treasure, this I know for sure. Through these temporary things (erudition, health, bodily vigour and so on), one cannot achieve that lasting goal. Yet by performing the Nachiketa sacrifice with these impermanent offerings, however, I have attained that which is Permanent.

Commentary:

This verse like many in the *Upanishad* is a kind of riddle. How can one through the transient gain the eternal? It means, "I have seen the *Nachiketa Agni* ritual whose nature is to give ephemeral results when performed as a material act. But when all our transient desires are themselves offered in the fire of renunciation (which is the example of Nachiketa), one can perform the same *Yajna* to achieve permanent and indestructible bliss." The soul becomes eternal for having sacrificed the ephemeral results of all *Karmas*. Not only material possessions but also their ephemeral benefits should be sacrificed. If God himself is saying these words, it relates to sacrifice of material desires even after *Yajna* performance, which has given the Gods their immortality and lasting power of wisdom. Gods accept offerings in *Yajnas*. Why? They grant material happiness to such seekers and wisdom to those who renounce such desires. The status of God, is a result of renouncing material pleasures. This is the secret of the *Nachiketa Agni* that releases one from all bondage.

11. *Kaamasyaaptim jagatah pratisthaam*
Kratoranantyam abhayasya paaram

Stomamahadurugaayam pratisthaam dristhvaa
Dhrityaa dheero Nachiketo atyasraaksheeh

Yama speaks Oh Nachiketa! Having seen the fulfillment of all desires, the support of the world, the endless fruit of rituals, you reached the other eternal shore beyond fear and have become strengthened by vision of that all-adorable ultimate.

Commentary:

The world is dependent on the ephemeral results of *Karma*. By rejecting them, Nachiketa has crossed over the limits of all mortality and entered into the region of fearlessness and truth, as a wise man.

12. *Tam durdarsam goodhamanupravistham*
Guhaahitam gahvarestham puraanam
Adhyaatma yogaadhigamena devam
Matvaa dheero harshasokau jahaati

Entering into that ultimate truth which cannot be envisioned, which is inscrutable, which is placed in the unapproachable region of the heart-cave, the ancient one - the wise, realising that it can only be obtained through the practice of *Dhyana Yoga* (meditation), knowing that, conquer the duality of happiness and sorrow.

Commentary:

The secret truth inside the Heart can be reached only through *Adhyatma* Yoga or inner Yoga, not by any ritual. Those who reach it can forever cross the duality of sorrow and happiness.

13. *Etat sritvaa samparigrihya martyah*
Pravrihya dharmya manumeta maapya
Sa modate modaneeyagm hi labdhvaa
Vivritagm sadma Nachiketasam manye

Any mortal, hearing this teaching and grasping its meaning, having comprehended this subtle *Dharma* realizes it, attains it and delights in all that is blissful. This sacred house of the ultimate, I hope, is opened for Nachiketa.

Commentary:

Receiving such a teaching, one should by *Tapas* attain the secret knowledge of the relationship between the *Jivatman* and *Paramatman*, the individual and the supreme. Only after that, can one attain true bliss.

14. *Anyatra dharmaadanyatraadharmaat*
Anyatraasmaat kritaakritaat
Anyatra bhootaaccha bhavyaaccha
Yattat pasyasi tadvada

Speak of that; what is other than Dharma and also other than Adharma, what is neither made nor unmade, what is different from the past and from the future, what one sees then.

Commentary:

Nachiketa has received the experience of the *Atman* from his Master. The Guru is asking him, as part of his teaching, to speak of that experience. This supreme experience is beyond all states of duality like Dharma and its opposite, Karma and its opposite and all divisions of time and space.

15. *Sarve vedaa yatpadamaamananti*
Tapaagmsi sarvaani cha yadvadanti
Yadicchanto brahmacharyam charanti
Tatte padagm sangrahena braveemyomityetat

The goal that all *Vedas* teach, the target or the fruit of all penance or *Tapas*, seeking which they practice *Brahmacharya* (austerities) — let me tell you about that briefly. That is *Om* (*Pranava*).

Commentary:

In his inimitable style of teaching, the God of Death asked Nachiketa to speak of his experience of the Self and now has answered the question himself that the total description of the experienced truth is *Om*. More than this, there are no words that could describe it.

16. *Etaddyevaaksharam Brahma*
Etaddyevaaksharam param
Etaddyevaakshram jnaatvaa
Yo yadicchati tasya tat

That imperishable syllable is *Brahman*. That imperishable syllable is the supreme. Those who know that imperishable syllable, what they wish for in that wisdom, that will be theirs.
Commentary:
An intense desire to achieve this realization results in *Tapas* leading to its attainment. This is achieved through meditation on *Om*.

17. *Etadaalambanagm srestham*
Etadaalambanam param
Etadaalambanam jnaatvaa
Brahmaloke maheeyate

This *Upasana* (or the practice of *Pranava*) is the greatest and dependable object for the seekers. By knowing this, with a thorough understanding of it and also by the internal experience (or realisation) one goes to the abode or state of *Brahman* (*Brahmaloka*).
Commentary:
This *Upasana* (or meditative practice of *Pranava-Om*) is the best object of dependence for seekers (*aalambanam*), who should constantly dwell upon it. Knowing it with a thorough understanding and by internal experience one goes to the abode or state of *Brahman*.

18. *Na jaayate mriyate vaa vipaschi*
Nnaayam kutaschinna babhoova kaschit
Ajo nityah saasvatoyam purano
Na hanyate hanyamaane sareere

The *Atma* is neither born nor dies. It does not have an origin. He (it) is unborn, eternal, constant and ancient. He is not destroyed when the body is destroyed.

Commentary:

Existing in mortal bodies, the Self does not experience living. It stands above the states of birth and death and pleasure and pain that the body suffers. It is the witness that knows all.

19. *Hantaa chenmanyate hantugm*
Hataschenmanyate hatam
Ubhau tau na vijaaneeto
Naayagm hanti na hanyate

If one thinks he is the slayer or the one who thinks he is slain, both do not know. The Self neither kills nor itself is killed since it exists in both the bodies unaffected.

20. *Anoraneeyaan mahato maheeyaan*
Aatmaasya jantornihito guhaayaam
Tamakratuh pasyati veetasoko
Dhaatuprasaadaanmahimaanamaatmanah

Smaller than the smallest and greater than the greatest, the Self is in the heart-cave of all creatures. One who is in his natural purity, beyond action, free of sorrow, perceives the majesty of that Self by the grace of God.

Commentary:

For such great achievement, the senses and sensuality must be subdued before this inner truth is experienced.

21. *Aaseeno dooram vrajati*
Sayaano yaati sarvatah
Kastam madaamadam devam
Madanyo jnaatu marhati

Sitting here, he travels far. Lying down, he reaches everywhere. Who other than myself is able to know that ecstatic state?

Commentary:

The state of a Yogi is that he in his soul or *Atman* can go far while sitting at one place and can travel anywhere, while lying down. Apart from any philosophical description of a universal consciousness, this *mantra* also indicates the achievements of Yogis, like travel in space or time. Of course, this also indicates the state of the knower of *Brahman* (*Brahma Jnani*) metaphorically since he is then a universal Self.

22. *Asariragm sareeresu*
Anavasthesvavasthitam
Mahaantam vibhumaatmaanam
Matvaa dheero na sochati

This *Atman* is bodiless though residing in numerous bodies. It has a changeless state while in the midst of all changing conditions. Realising this *Atman* as the all-pervasive supreme entity, the brave and wise do not grieve.

23. *Naayamaatmaa pravachanena labhyo*
Na medhayaa na bahunaa srutena
Yamevaisa vrinute tena labhyah
Tasyaisa atmaa vivrinute tanoogm svaam

The *Atman* is not obtained by mere verbal discourse, or by any intellectual acumen or even by much listening. The Self reveals its own nature, on its own when the individual transcends ignorance.

Commentary:

The futility of mere mental learning is once more stressed. The only real approach to the higher Self is through *Tapas*, when it reveals itself by choosing such a one who is sincerely in search of it.

24. *Naavirato duscharitaan*
Naasaanto naasamaahitah
Naasaantamaanaso vapi
Prajnaanenainamaapnuyaat

One who has not diverted himself from bad behaviour, who is not peaceful and whose senses are uncontrolled, one who has no tranquil mind - such a one does not have the insight to reach the Self. One can obtain it only through right awareness (*Prajna*).

25. *Yasya brahma cha kshatram cha*
Ubhe bhavata odanah
Mrityuryasyopasechanam
Ka itthaa veda yatra sah

That one for whom both the paths of *Brahmana* and active royal power (*Kshatra*), are becoming a meal, and are served as light food through the nature's Law of death, who knows where such a one (*Atman*) is present?

Commentary:

Here, death is described as the supreme *Brahman* itself. The ignorant undergo the experience of death and the wise experience immortality from one and the same source. There are no two such things as Death and Immortality existing separately. Only one truth of *Atman* exists. The Vedic path of the ritualistic *Brahmin* or the worldly activity of the *Kshatriya* (prince), are both ephemeral and therefore food for this God of Death.

(This entire section is an unequivocal and emphatic assertion that *Tapas* is the only path to *Atman* or *Brahman*.)

* * *

Third Section — TRITEEYA VALLI

1. *Rtam pibantau sukritasya loke*
Guhaam pravishtau parame paraardhe
Chayaatapau Brahmavido vadanti
Panchaagnayo ye cha trinaachiketaah

The knowers of *Brahman*, who have worshipped the five fires and performed the Nachiketa ritual, having drunk the essence of virtuous deeds enter the cave of heart that is placed in the highest realm, speak of the two, light and shadow (the *Jivatman* and *Paramatman*).

Commentary:

Two kinds of souls are described here. Those who by good deeds go to higher worlds; and those who enter the secret cave in the heart-centre by Yoga, which is higher than the highest world. A subtle difference is made between the souls dwelling in the higher worlds and those who reach the centre of creation within the heart.

The light here emanates from the *Brahman* and illumines the happiness of the souls. *Panchaagnayo* are those who have controlled the five *Pranas* through Yoga and by ascending through *Sushumna* have reached the Heart-centre. *Trinaachiketaagnayah* indicates those who have reached the higher worlds through the merits of mere ritual, whose happiness while living in the higher worlds is but a shadow of happiness. These two are like the light and shadow. The relative status of mere *Karma* and the ultimate Yoga are once again indicated here.

There is no end to the literature that supports this theory. When the *Jivatman* is able to pierce the *Chakras* and has vision of the *Paramatman* within, it loses its state of Jivahood. This is equated to *Saameepya*, *Saalokya* and even *Saaroopya* (having proximity to, the same higher world or the same form as the Lord). It is necessary therefore for the *Jivatman* to reach a point of proximity to the *Paramatman*. The science of Yoga prescribes the method of piercing through this wonderful, mystic and great heart centre.

Here a subtle difference between the two kinds of people dwelling in higher worlds and those reaching the centre of creation within is made out.

Another interpretation is that the '*Panchaagnayah*' and '*Trinaachiketah*' are those who perform both '*Nachiketa*' as a ritual and also follow the path of Yoga knowing the secret of the five *pranas* within, as taught in this *Upanishad*. They are in the pure reality of *Brahman*. So say the knowers of *Brahman*.

2. *Yah setureejaanaanaam*
   Aksharam Brahmayatparam
   Abhayam titeershataam paaram
   Naachiketagm sakemahi

Which is a bridge that connects the ritualist with the imperishable *Brahman* that is the supreme, which leads to the other shore beyond fear for those seeking to go beyhond this world, may we perform that Nachiketa ritual only.

Commentary:

This *mantra* indicates the *Pratijna* the commitment to the path consequent to such a situation. The Nachiketa ritual should be performed with *Upasana* or inner meditative worship. Then it becomes capable of bridging *Karma* and *Tapas*.

3. *Aatmaanagm rathinam viddhi*
   Sariragm rathameva tu
   Buddhim tu saarathim viddhi
   Manah pragraha meva cha

Yama said: Know that *Atman*, the Self, as the rider and body as the chariot which he rides. Know the intellect (*Buddhi*) as the driver of the chariot and the mind (*Manas*) as the controlling reins.

Commentary:

The soul moves about in the chariot of the body, which is driven according to the commands of the intellect or *Buddhi*. It functions with the outer or sensory mind (*Manas*) holding the reins of the horses that constitute the sensory and motor organs.

4. *Indriyaani hayaanaahuh*
   Vishayaagmstesu gocharaan
   Aatmendriya manoyuktam
   Bhoktetyaahuh maneeshinah

The wise, compare the senses with horses and the sense objects with their field of travel. The charioteer is becoming the *Bhokta* or enjoyer of the sensual experiences (due to ignorance.)

Commentary:

The soul connected to the mind and senses becomes the apparent enjoyer (*Bhokta*) in the world of *Samsara.*

5. *Yastvavijnaanavaan bhavati*
   Ayuktena manasaa sadaa
   Tasyendriyaani avasyaani
   Dusthaasvaa iva saaratheh

He who is ignorant, ever with an uncontrolled mind, whose senses are out of his control, he is like the foolish driver with wild horses.

6. *Yastu vijnaanavaan bhavati*
   Yuktena manasaa sadaa
   Tasyendriyaani vasyaani
   Sadasvaa iva saaratheh

He who has true knowledge, ever with a controlled mind,

whose senses are in his control, he is like a wise driver with good horses.

7. *Yastvavijnaanavaan bhavati*
Amanaskah sadaa asuchih
Na sa tatpadamaapnoti
Sagmsaaram cha adhigacchati

He who is ignorant, with an uncontrolled mind and ever impure inside, he cannot attain the Ultimate. He remains in *Samsara*.

8. *Yastu vijnaanavaan bhavati*
Samanaskah sadaa suchih
Sa tu tatpadamaapnoti
Yasmaadbhooyo na jaayate

He who has strong intention for liberation, with a controlled mind, who is ever pure inside, conquers ignorance and he attains the Ultimate from which he is not further born again.

9. *Vijnaana saarathiryastu*
Manah pragrahavaannarah
So adhvanah paaramaapnoti
Tadvishnoh paramam padam

The man who has commissioned his *Buddhi* (discriminating intellect) as the driver of his body, who holds his mind as the reins of the horse-like senses, he reaches the ultimate goal, the culmination of spiritual path, the supreme abode of *Vishnu*.

10. *Indriyebhyah paraahyarthaa*
Arthebhyascha param manah
Manasastu paraa buddhih
Buddheraatmaa mahaanparah

The sense-objects are subtler than the sense organs. The mind (*Manas*) is greater or subtler than the sense objects. The intellect (*Buddhi*) is greater than the mind and *Atman* is ultimate.

Commentary:

Manas is the outer mind connected to the senses. *Buddhi* is the inner mind that discriminates. The great *Atman*, *Mahan atman* is supreme *Brahman*.

11. *Mahatah paramavyaktam*
Avyaktaatpurusah parah
Purusaanna param kinchit
Saa kaasthaa saa paraa gatih

Subtler than *Mahat* (universal mind) is *Avyakta* or the Unmanifest. Beyond *Avyakta* is the *Purusha*. He is the ultimate and the supreme goal. There is nothing beyond Him. One who realises this truth is attaining that ultimate.

Commentary:

This section reflects the basic theory of *Sankhya* and its main *tattvas* upon which the science of Yoga is built. These *Mantras* from 3 to 12 are also discussed in commentaries on the *Brahma Sutras*.

The *Brahma Sutras* have asserted that the *Avyakta* in this *mantra* indicates *Maya* (which is inherent in Brahman or Purusha) but not *Pradhana* of the *Sankhyas* (which is posited as an independent principle to the Purusha). If *Avyakta* indicates the unmanifest subtle cause of creation, the *Sankhya* assertion that it is '*Achetana*' or 'adynamic' can be modified by Yoga's complementary theory, which propounds the *Isvara* as the primary cause. This would take us to the view that *Avyakta* together with *Isvara* and *Mahat* are approximately synonymous.

12. *Esha sarvesu bhootesu*
Goodho aatmaa na prakaasate
Drisyate tvagryayaa buddhyaa
Sookshmayaa sookshma darsibhih

That Self, though latent witness in all beings is not visible by itself. It is seen only by a very keen and subtle intellect, subtle vision, concentration and attention. That is *Tapas* alone.

13. *Yacchedvaagmanasee prajnah*
Tadyacchet jnaana aatmani
Jnaanamaatmani mahati niyacchet
Tadyacchet saanta aatmani

The man of discrimination should merge speech into the mind; mind into the sense of discrimination; discrimination into the greater self and the greater self into the tranquil *Atman*.

14. *Uttisthata jaagrata*
Praapya varaannibodhata
Kshurasyadhaaraa nisitaa duratyayaa
Durgam patham tatkavayo vadanti

Oh Nachiketa! Arise and awake; having obtained your desired boons, attain the realisation of the supreme *Brahman*. As sharp as the edge of a razor and difficult to pass over — such is the difficult path that the seers declare.

15. *Asabda masparsa maroopa mavyayam*
Tathaa rasam nitya magandhavaccha yat
Anaadyanantam mahatah param dhrivam
Nichaayya tam mrityumukhaatpramuchyate

That which cannot be heard or touched, which has no form and is undiminishing, that which has no taste or smell and is eternal. That, which has no beginning or end, magnificent, beyond all and ever constant—those who have experienced this are liberated from the mouth of death.

16. *Naachiketamupaakhyaanam*
Mrityuproktagm sanaatanam
Uktvaa srutvaacha medhaavi
Brahmaloke maheeyate

This ancient story of Nachiketa, told by the God of Death Himself, when spoken or heard by the wise, has the capacity to take one to *Brahma Loka*.

17. *Ya imam paramam guhyam*
Sraavayet brahmasamsadi
Prayatah sraaddhakaale vaa
Tadaanantyaaya kalpate
Tadaanantyaaya kalpata iti

Those who hear this supreme secret paying great attention in a congregation of the wise, or at the ceremonial rites conducted for the dead, become eligible for liberation, reach the limitless truth.

Om Santih

A General Commentary on Vallis IV to VI

In this Second Chapter or *Adhyaya* (containing three *Vallis* — fourth, fifth and sixth), specifically in the sixth and seventh *mantras* of the fourth *Valli*, it has been stressed that the *Paramatman* dwells in the cave of the heart and it is the Creator of the Gods. But in the individual's heart, the *Atman* wears the image of a man, *Angusthamaatrah purusah madhye Atmani tisthati* (*Atmani* - one's own self), (*Valli*-4, *mantra*-12). In *mantra*-13, (*Angusthamaatrah puruso jyotirivaadhoomakah*) it is again stressed that it is a 'body of light' without smoke.

To say that this is a *Yoga Upanishad*, we may find evidence in the 3rd *mantra* of 5th *Valli* also:

Uoordhvam Prana munnayatyapaanam pratyagasyati
Madhye vaamanamaaseenam visvedevaa upaasate

Directing the *Prana* upwards and taking the *Apana* down, the dwarf (*Vamana* or the inch-man) that is seated in the heart-centre, all the Gods worship him.

The *mantra* 4 of the 5th *Valli* reads:

Asya visramsamaanasya sarirasthasya dehinah
Dehaadvimuchyamaanasya kimatra parisisyate
Etat vai tat

What remains of this wandering soul placed in the body when he is liberated from the body; This is That.

Mantra 5 of the 5th *Valli* reads:

Na praanena na apaanena martyo jeevati kaschana
Itarena tu jeevanti yasminnetaa upaasritau

No mortal lives by mere inhalation (*Prana*) or exhalation (*Apana*), but by the strength of *Atman*, which is responsible for the *pranas* to function.

Iha chedasakat boddhum prak sareerasya visrasah
Tatah sargesu lokesu sareeratvaaya kalpathe

This is an interesting *mantra* (6.4) which refers to a Yogi (or one with merit earned otherwise), taking his birth in the higher worlds. It says, if one has not realised the *Brahman*, but is freed from *Prakriti* on earth before he leaves his body in this world, even if a merited soul, he has to take repeated births until he is freed from an ego-consciousness. In *mantra* (6.5), it is described how one sees the *Atman* in oneself:

Yathaa darse tathaa aatmani
Yathaa svapne tathaa pitruloke
Yathaapsu pareevadadrise tathaa Gandharvaloke
Chaayaatapayoriva Brahmaloke

For a man here on earth the vision of *Atman* is like in a mirror. This is significantly indicative of the fact that *Atman* is located at the centre of the Heart and its reflection is in the core of the Self — *Jivatman* or *Angustha Purusha*. Its vision is its realisation. It is like a mirror reflection. In the higher worlds however there is no gross body like that of the human being and hence no *Angustha Purusha*. Still, a more spiritual, subtler body — known as the *Divya Sarira* — is worn by the *Jivatman*. If it is *Pitru Loka* — world of manes — the Self is seen like in a dream. It is more vague than in the human body. In the *Gandharva Loka*, it is seen like a reflection in water. In *Brahma Loka* it is seen like a light and shadow. This indicates that the *Atman's* reflection in human body is as clear as in a mirror, and thus the human body is most eminently suited for self-realisation. This *Antaratman* or *Angustha Purusha* is always close to the Heart (*Sannivisthah* - close proximity).

In the *mantra* 11 of the last (6th) *Valli*, again the word 'Yoga' has been used saying that the merger of the senses into the *Atman* is 'Yoga'. Mere words and thoughts cannot take one to its experience. One must go beyond the mind and senses.

In the *mantras* 14, 15 and 16 of the last *Valli*, the state of *Samadhi* is described. All the knots around the Heart-centre are pierced. There are 101 Nadis at the Heart-centre leading to the centre of the pericarp. The Yogi who follows the path of that one Nadi, which reaches the ultimate point in the pericarp in order to leave the body, can free himself from rebirth. The others who live and leave through the other *Nadis* take a rebirth in different realms.

In *mantra* 17, the *Angusthamaatra Purusha* is said to be close to the *Antaratman* near the Heart-centre. '*Sadaa sannivisthah*' may also mean that *Atman* is always inside the subtle body. They have to be discriminated apart. The *Atman* must be separated from the body and its image in the body. It must be directly experienced.

In *mantra* 18, it is unequivocally stressed that it is possible to know the *Atman* only through 'Yoga' and by no other means. This *Upanishad* is, therefore, clearly a *Yoga Upanishad*, and had special Yoga practices taught along with it. While it often stresses the vedantic truths about the human body, the *Atman* and the *Paramatman*, in accordance with the other *Upanishads*, it is pointing to the single, ultimate *Brahman* only. In this way it contains the essence of both Yoga and Vedanta as a single, succinct, practical teaching, with the authority of the God Himself.

Read this commentary again and again
and conquer your death

OM TATSAT

Index

Bibliography

1. Yoga Sutras of Patanjali
2. Shatchakra Niroopanam — Commentary by Arthur Avlon and Many Others
3. Taittiriya Brahmana
4. Krishna Yajurveda Taittiriyaaranyaka Bhagah
5. Commentaries on Panchakathakas of Krishna Yajurveda
6. Suresvara's Vartika on Asvamedha Brahmana
7. Sankara's Commentary on the Brihadaranyaka Upanishad
8. Brihadaranyaka Vartikasara by Vidyaranya
9. Kathopanishad — Commentaries by Shri Sankara and Many Others
10. Paadma Samhita
11. Rudra Adhyaya
12. Bhagavadgita

Diacritical Markings — Pronunciation

Vowels

अ a आ ā इ i ई ī उ u ऊ ū ऋ ṛ ॠ ṝ

ऌ lṛ ए e ऐ ai ओ o औ au

ṁ (anusvāra) ḥ (visarga)

Consonants

Gutturals:	क **ka**	ख **kha**	ग **ga**	घ **gha**	ङ **ṅa**
Palatals:	च **ca**	छ **cha**	ज **ja**	झ **jha**	ञ **ña**
Cerebrals:	ट **ṭa**	ठ **ṭha**	ड **ḍa**	ढ **ḍha**	ण **ṇa**
Dentals:	त **ta**	थ **tha**	द **da**	ध **dha**	न **na**
Labials :	प **pa**	फ **pha**	ब **ba**	भ **bha**	म **ma**
Semivowels:	य **ya**	र **ra**	ल **la**	व **va**	
Sibilants:	श **śa**	ष **ṣa**	स **sa**		
Aspirate:	ह **ha**		ऽ = ’ (avagraha) - the apostrophe		